# IMAGINING

## — THE —

# FUTURE

# Dedication

To Tessa Torok – ST

To Kate and Sarah Holper – PH

# Acknowledgements

Thanks to Andrew and Mitzi Forgas, Matilda Torok, John Stewart and Sarah Holper for ideas, Paul Torok for school student input, and Scott Power for statistical assistance. Thank you to Kath Kovac, Janet and Sarah Holper, Helen Doyle and Russell Cockman for helpful review comments. And thanks to Briana Melideo at CSIRO Publishing for her ideas and guidance.

# IMAGINING

## — THE —

# FUTURE

### Invisibility, Immortality and 40 Other Incredible Ideas

## Simon Torok and Paul Holper

CSIRO

PUBLISHING

National Library of Australia Cataloguing-in-Publication entry

Torok, Simon, author.

Imagining the future : invisibility, immortality and 40 other incredible ideas / Simon Torok and Paul Holper.

9781486302727 (paperback)
9781486302734 (epdf)
9781486302741 (epub)

For ages 9–13.

Technological innovations – Juvenile literature.
Inventions – Juvenile literature.
Science – Juvenile literature.

Holper, Paul N., 1957– author.

600

Published by

CSIRO Publishing
Locked Bag 10
Clayton South VIC 3169
Australia

Telephone: +61 3 9545 8400
Email: publishing.sales@csiro.au
Website: www.publish.csiro.au

Illustrations by Thomson Digital

Set in 9.5/13 Helvetica Neue
Edited by Dr Kath Kovac
Cover design by Alicia Freile, Tango Media
Text design and typeset by James Kelly
Printed in China by 1010 Printing International Ltd

CSIRO Publishing publishes and distributes scientific, technical and health science books, magazines and journals from Australia to a worldwide audience and conducts these activities autonomously from the research activities of the Commonwealth Scientific and Industrial Research Organisation (CSIRO). The views expressed in this publication are those of the author(s) and do not necessarily represent those of, and should not be attributed to, the publisher or CSIRO. The copyright owner shall not be liable for technical or other errors or omissions contained herein. The reader/user accepts all risks and responsibility for losses, damages, costs and other consequences resulting directly or indirectly from using this information.

**Original print edition:** The paper this book is printed on is in accordance with the rules of the Forest Stewardship Council®. The FSC® promotes environmentally responsible, socially beneficial and economically viable management of the world's forests.

# Foreword

## THE FUTURE IS AWESOME, IT'S ALREADY HERE AND IT JUST KEEPS GETTING BETTER.

Scientific journals are packed with evidence to support this optimism, but here's my favourite example. When I started working in the laser industry as a young physicist, the idea of growing a crystal that efficiently converts electrical energy to bright blue light seemed like a distant – if not impossible – dream. Less than 20 years later, three Japanese scientists shared the Nobel Prize in Physics for making this quantum mechanical magic trick come true. Their invention, the blue light-emitting diode, now illuminates the colour screen on your smart phone, computer and a kazillion other devices you interact with every day. I even own a blue laser diode, and it's impossible to exaggerate how amazing that is.

The future promises a treasure trove of incredible discoveries: from the nature of dark energy and dark matter to unimagined new materials, from faster computers and novel nanotechnology to unprecedented amounts of 'big data', from remote sensors to the Internet of Things, from cleaner energy to better medicine and healthcare – and much, much more amazingness that simply cannot be predicted today.

But there is an 'if' to all this optimism, and it's a big one. We need more kids to get hooked on science and mathematics – and to believe in their own ability to make these dreams come true. Simon and Paul are expert guides to this fantastic future. This terrific book will teach you how to dream big while keeping both your feet planted firmly on the ground.

Enjoy the ride!

**Ruben Meerman**
ABC's Surfing Scientist

# Contents

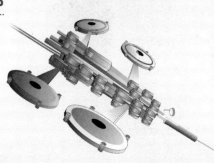

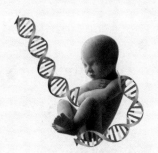

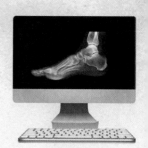

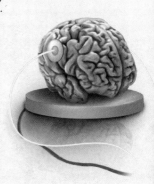

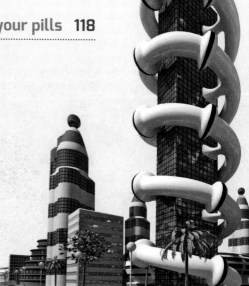

# Are you ready for the future?

We're living in a rapidly changing world. Around the year 1900, the amount of human knowledge doubled every 100 years. It now doubles almost every year, and by 2020 could double every day. This means that a lot of what students starting a university degree learn in their first year will be outdated by the time they finish. When most of today's students in primary school grow up, they'll have jobs that don't exist right now. They'll be using technologies that haven't been invented to solve things that we don't know are problems yet.

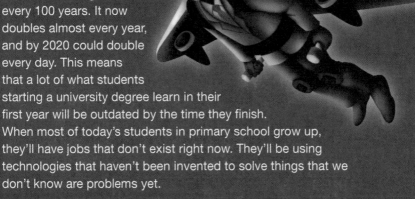

So you need to be ready – and this handbook for the future will help you. Reading it will be like time travelling.

Some inventions we thought were impossible when we started planning this book are now close to reality. Some of it really freaked us out! We would write about a cool idea – such as hoverboards or driverless cars – only to read about them in the news a few weeks later, already invented.

Time flies, but science soars. Things that seemed impossible a generation ago are now commonplace. When your parents were young, making a phone call meant sitting in one place inside the house, talking into a telephone wired via a plug to the outside world. The thought of making a call from the beach, the top of a mountain or a car was crazy. Today's mobile phones are not only portable; they do a lot more than just make calls.

Other inventions common today that seemed like science fiction just decades ago include instant electronic communication all around the world, a station in space visited by reusable spacecraft, 3D colour television and a pill to cure polio.

In the past, some imaginative people envisaged inventions that we take for granted today. In 1964, science fiction author Isaac Asimov wrote about what he thought would be a reality by 2014. He correctly predicted that appliances would not use electric cords, instead being powered by longlife batteries. He envisaged that many routine jobs would be performed by machines. And he predicted that life expectancy would reach 85 years due to medical technologies. But he incorrectly thought that there would be cities beneath the sea and colonies on the Moon, and that flying cars would make roads outdated.

Many others from the past failed to foresee the future. In 1895, the president of the British Royal Society said that 'heavier-than-air flying machines are impossible'. A senior United States film studio producer predicted in 1946 that television wouldn't last, because 'people will soon get tired of staring at a plywood box every night'. And in 1977, the chairperson of the Digital Equipment Corporation said 'there is no reason for any individual to have a computer in their home'. Don't they all look like chumps now?

Then there are inventions that we probably don't want to see. In the 1960s, people predicted that by the year 2000, food would come out of a tube or be in the form of a tablet. In 1955, vacuum cleaner company president Alex Lewitt predicted that a nuclear-powered vacuum cleaner would be 'a reality within 10 years'. Luckily, they were wrong.

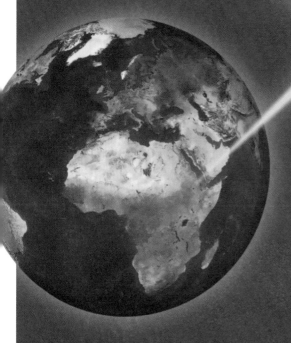

Nonetheless, realistic predictions of the future and the far-fetched imaginings of science fiction can inspire ideas. As you'll read in this book, invisibility, immunity, instant transportation, holograms and many other ideas and gadgets appeared in books and movies long before they were developed in the real world. You'll be surprised how close to reality some science fiction ideas have become. Who knows – you may be involved in making the final discoveries that lead to a dream becoming a reality!

If you do try to turn your dreams into reality, it's OK to fail. When it comes to inventions and innovation, any failure is a lesson along the pathway to success. Thomas Edison, who created the electric light bulb and many other inventions, said 'I have not failed. I've just found 10 000 ways that won't work.'

We need to dream. Dreams help us imagine the future. And imagining the future is the first step in arriving there. If you can dream it, perhaps one day you can invent it.

We hope this book will help you determine when science fiction will become science fact.

**Simon Torok** and **Paul Holper**

'THE WORLD IS MOVING SO FAST THESE DAYS THAT THE MAN WHO SAYS IT CAN'T BE DONE IS GENERALLY INTERRUPTED BY SOMEONE DOING IT.'

– ELBERT HUBBARD

# BEING
# TRANSPARENT

WHAT TRICKS
COULD YOU PLAY
ON YOUR FRIENDS
IF YOU WERE
INVISIBLE?

We all love the idea of being able to creep around, watching people without them knowing, eavesdropping on conversations. Think of all the fun you could have if, at the snap of a finger, you could become invisible.

Lots of books and movies have featured people who deliberately or accidentally became invisible, such as *The Invisible Man* and *Harry Potter*. In some stories, experiments with chemicals and nuclear explosions have made fictional characters become see-through.

## Invisible ship

There are also tales of real-life objects being made invisible. Perhaps the most famous is the 'Philadelphia Experiment'. In 1943, during World War II, so the story goes, the United States Navy fitted a mass of electronic equipment on a small ship, the *USS Eldridge*. They were trying to create huge magnetic fields that would bend light and radio waves around the ship, so that enemies couldn't see it.

The experiment was done at the Philadelphia dockyard and at sea. Apparently, within minutes of the power being turned on, people saw a thick, green fog slowly surround the ship. Within minutes, the fog disappeared. The *USS Eldridge* had vanished! About 15 minutes later, navy officers shut down the generators. The fog slowly reappeared, bringing the ship back into view.

The United States Navy claims that this experiment never happened – the story is just an urban myth, or a hoax. But the military can indeed make things invisible – to radar.

## Real-life invisibility

'Stealth' aircraft have radar-absorbing panels and are painted with a special coating. This deflects radar signals up or down, rather than back to the radar-detecting instrument, making it harder for the radar to detect objects.

A team from the University of Singapore has developed an invisibility gun. It makes things invisible by bathing them in a beam of darkness. Using a laser and a special lens, the researchers have used the darkness beam to hide a tiny three-dimensional model of the letter 'N'. The method works only with small objects, so the challenge for the researchers will be scaling it up to the size of a person – if they really want it to catch on.

An English company has used tiny carbon tubes called nanotubes, each 10 000 times thinner than a human hair, to make a material they claim is blacker than black. The material captures 99.96 per cent of the light that hits it. When coated onto aluminium foil, it makes the foil almost impossible to see. 'It's like black, like a hole, like there's nothing there,' says a company spokesperson.

A nanotube material called Vantablack will be used in astronomical cameras and telescopes to reduce the reflections from stray light. This will let astronomers spot faint stars. If you could make a shirt from Vantablack, it would appear as if your head was floating in mid air, with your hands suspended nearby. Could this be just like the Harry Potter cloak of invisibility?

Invisibility is also likely to have medical benefits. For example, invisible skin could help doctors during operations. Researchers in Texas in the United States have made small areas of rat or hamster skin nearly transparent for at

least 20 minutes. They did this by injecting a clear, sticky liquid called glycerol into the animal's skin. They could then see through the skin to the blood vessels underneath.

If used on people, this 'invisible skin' technique would allow doctors to more accurately focus laser beams during operations. The technology could also have lots of applications for medical diagnosis (for example, identifying diseases) and new treatments for illnesses.

## Can we become invisible?

An invisible person may not be such a big deal, if some astronomers turn out to be correct. They have identified what they believe to be invisible planets and invisible stars, made of 'mirror matter'. But how do astronomers see objects that are invisible?
They do it by observing the 'wobbles' made by visible planets and stars, and working out which additional, odd movements must have been caused by the gravity of invisible objects.

If all else fails, you could put on purple clothes and stand still against a purple wall. It will make you more difficult to see, but of course, this is not being invisible. This is just using camouflage.

# ETERNITY

## Living forever

**COULD WE EVER BECOME IMMORTAL?**

**People now live longer than ever before. A girl born in Australia today can expect to live for about 84 years, but a girl born in the late 1800s was expected to live for just 54 years.**

We owe this improvement to better food, advances in medicine and having more money. Fewer babies and young children die, and our work and lives are far safer than they used to be.

## Long life

Jeanne Calment lived to 122. Born on 21 February 1875 in Arles, France, she was 28 when Orville Wright became the first person to fly a powered plane. When she was 94, Neil Armstrong walked on the Moon. Jeanne lived through two world wars, the invention of television and the birth of the internet.

She remembered selling pencils to the famous Dutch artist, Vincent Van Gogh, in her father's shop.

How long you live, or your longevity, can be influenced by where you are born. While Arles seems like a good choice, top of the ladder is actually nearby Monaco, where the average baby is likely to live to almost 90. Macau, Japan and Singapore follow. Australia ranks 10th worldwide in longevity, while babies born in the African country, Chad, have the shortest life expectancy – just 49 years.

Humans live longer than most animals, but there are exceptions. For instance, a Galapagos tortoise named Harriet died at Australia Zoo in Queensland in 2006. Keepers said that she was 176 years old. Bowhead whales can live about 200 years, and clams even longer: researchers discovered a 507-year-old deep-sea clam off the coast of Iceland.

Jellyfish have come up with a novel way of making their lives longer. A species called *Turritopsis dohrnii* can reverse its life cycle. It's been called the 'immortal jellyfish'; being immortal means living forever. The jellyfish switches back and forth between its adult stage and its young form, called a polyp – just like in the movie *17 Again*. How would you like to be five years old again?

Plants can live extremely long lives. A yew tree growing in Britain is thought to be up to 5000 years old. A quaking aspen tree in Colorado, United States, has a root system that's more than 80 000 years old.

While an amoeba or a bacterium lives, it ages like every other living thing. But eventually it divides, forming two identical copies of itself, called daughter cells. The two daughter cells can be thought of as young copies of the parent cell. So the original amoeba or bacterium can be around for a long, long time.

## Steps to living longer

What can be done to extend your life? Let's start with the things you can control yourself.

First: watch your diet and weight. The Mediterranean area of Europe is home to lots of people who are more than 100 years old. Most people there eat healthy diets that are high in fruits, vegetables, nuts and healthy fats such as olive oil. Also, don't smoke or drink too much alcohol when you are older.

Next: study. Educated people live longer. They are more likely to have better jobs and make healthier lifestyle choices. Be friendly. Strong social networks help support us; helping other people may help us better look after ourselves.

Exercise is good. Light physical activity every day leads to less disability in old age and a longer, healthier life. Stand instead of sitting. Sitting for long periods when studying, working and watching television is unhealthy, so try to spend some time doing these things on your feet.

## Inside your cells

Researchers have managed to make laboratory worms live for five times longer than worms living in nature. If this research could be applied to us, we'd be living to 500. Our body is, of course, far more complex than a worm's body.

The scientists did this by making two helpful changes to the worms' genes, which control the nature of new cells. They are now trying to see if they can make mice live longer, too.

Just like bacterial cells, our cells must also reproduce by dividing into new daughter cells. This is how we grow new skin, tissues, blood and bone. Within our cells, the DNA of our genes is arranged into structures called

chromosomes. At the ends of the chromosomes are stretches of DNA called telomeres. The telomeres protect our genes by helping cells make accurate copies of themselves.

Elizabeth Blackburn, from Tasmania, jointly won the 2009 Nobel Prize with Carol Greider and Jack Szostak for research into telomeres and the enzymes that create them. Enzymes are proteins that do lots of jobs in a cell, such as helping to build other proteins or breaking down unwanted material.

Elizabeth and her team found that just like the plastic tips on shoelaces, telomeres help keep the chromosome chains from being damaged. As we age, our telomeres start getting shorter, meaning that our chromosomes get damaged and that our cells can no longer copy themselves as accurately. If the telomeres in a cell are too short, then the cell may die. Some inherited diseases (a disease someone is born with) involve faulty telomeres, resulting in damaged cells.

The enzyme that makes the telomeres is called telomerase. So the question is, can telomerase protect or restore the length of the telomeres that cap the end of chromosomes? Could it make us live longer by stopping our cells from aging? Genetic scientist Richard Cawthon and his colleagues at the University of Utah, in the United States, say 'yes'. They believe that if we could stop telomeres from shortening, we could add 10 to 30 years to our lives.

## Grandpa avatar

If the longlife scientists fail, perhaps next best is to do what the bacteria do and clone yourself – or at least, some parts of yourself.

Companies are seeking to create personalised, conscious 'avatar' robots. An avatar is a representation of a person. The idea is that the avatar robot will look like you and perhaps even speak like you. Loaded into its memory will be snippets of your life – photos, videos and letters or emails you have sent or received.

The asking price is $500 000 for a fairly basic version of an avatar robot. Wealthy folk might jump at the chance to be able to pass on some details of their lives to great-great-great-grandchildren. But it's certainly not living forever.

# SKY-HIGHWAY

**Flying cars**

WOULD YOU LIKE TO AVOID TRAFFIC IN A FLYING CAR?

For decades people have dreamed of cars that fly through the air. They could soar above traffic jams without the bulk of an aeroplane's wide wingspan, or the need to be stuck at an airport.

In the 1960s, flying cars were popular in fiction. *The Jetsons*, a cartoon family living in the year 2062, travelled by flying car. The 1989 film *Back to the Future Part II*, set in 2015, had flying cars and hoverboards. In more recent movies, Harry Potter travelled to Hogwarts aboard the Weasleys' flying car, while Lucy Wilde's car had extendable wings that enabled a quick getaway in *Despicable Me 2*.

## Keys to the real world

Flying cars are almost as old as flying aeroplanes, but none have really made it past the test stage to become widely available. In 1917, less than 15 years after the Wright brothers flew the first aeroplane at Kittyhawk in the United States, Glenn Curtiss invented a car with three wings and a propeller.

Robert Fulton tried something different in 1946. Instead of modifying a car to make a plane, he modified a plane into a car. His 'Airphibian' could be converted into a car in five minutes by removing the wings, tail and propeller. The following year, plans to build 160 000 cars with a huge wing, propeller and tail were abandoned after a crash when it ran out of fuel. Although the pilot had checked the car's fuel gauge, the separate propeller engine's tank was empty.

Henry Ford predicted in 1940 that 'a combination airplane and motorcar is coming.' He worked with engineers in the Ford company's aircraft division to develop the first 'aerocar'. The result was the Ford Flivver, a single-seat plane that could be driven along a road. However, the prototype was described by famous pilot Charles Lindbergh as one of the worst planes he'd ever flown. Furthermore, the Flivver's test pilot was killed in a crash off the Florida coast, which stopped the small plane's development. Henry Ford declared in the 1950s that, 'the day where there will be an aerocar in every garage is still some time off.'

## Flying towards the future

In recent years, aircraft with names such as the Sparrowhawk, Airscooter II, and the Personal Air and Land Vehicle have been commercially available. But these look more like helicopters or ultra-light planes than flying cars.

The Terrafugia company's Transition vehicle is referred to as a 'roadable aircraft' rather than a flying car. It has wings that fold up, enabling it to share the road with cars. The Moller Skycar is known as a 'personal vertical take-off and landing aircraft'. But these haven't cracked the personal car market, so while flying cars may have got off the ground literally, the companies have failed to do so financially.

The flying car you'll most likely first see in your neighbourhood is the AeroMobil. A video of the prototype is online and the company claims the AeroMobil is ready for production. Designed in Slovakia, a country in Europe, it is also referred to as a roadable aircraft, because it has wings that fold back to transform the plane into what looks like a futuristic sports car. It can fly at 200 kilometres per hour for more than 700 kilometres, land to fill up at a petrol station, and fit into a car parking space.

If you don't have your driver's licence, maybe the *Back to the Future* film's hoverboard will do. Arx Pax in the United States has developed a prototype flying skateboard called the Hendo Hover. Four disc-shaped magnetic engines enable it to support a person a couple of centimetres above the ground. The prototype costs around $11 000.

## Dude, where's my flying car?

Flying cars are considered to signal the arrival of the future – or rather, the lack of its arrival. They have been promised by inventors for decades, and always seem to be just around the corner, but have never become commercially available.

Mass-produced flying cars are still not likely to be around the next bend. They face many possible problems. Stopping on the side of the road when you break down or run out of petrol would be likely to be a fatal exercise in

a flying car. Fears of flying could reduce their popularity, and a pilot's licence is a lot harder to obtain than a driver's licence. It's also unlikely that they'll be affordable for most of us – even if mass produced, they will probably cost hundreds of thousands of dollars (around 10 times the price of a normal car). And flying in bad weather may not be possible.

Despite these problems, the National Aeronautics and Space Administration (NASA) recently completed a study about making more use of the roughly 3000 small airports in the United States. Perhaps advances in design and engineering, the development of new lightweight materials, and computer-assisted flying may make the flying car a possibility . . . if not for you, perhaps by the time your children get their licences.

# FASTER FOOD

## 3D printed food

HOW WOULD YOU LIKE TO PRINT YOUR DINNER?

You arrive home from school, hungry for a snack. You feel like something different; not the usual food your fridge and pantry automatically order based on what you normally eat. So you search for a treat on the internet, find one that looks good, and press print. Your 3D printer creates a ready-to-eat copy. Meanwhile, your parents are in the kitchen printing dinner.

Welcome to the high-speed, low-waste, good-health world of future food.

## Entree

3D printers were invented in the 1980s. Rather than print an image using a layer of ink, they can print an object using layers of plastic or metal. Through the 1990s and 2000s, 3D printing helped in the design of new products and was used to make one-off prototypes of objects. Today, 3D printers are cheaper and more widely available. They are already used in mass production of items in factories and to print objects at home.

It is early days for 3D food printing. You can buy a 3D chocolate printer, which uses melted chocolate to print chocolate pictures and objects. Similarly, a sugar-based 3D printer can print sweets in creative shapes. A 3D pasta printer can print ravioli if you top up its 'printer cartridge' with dough and filling. Other 3D printers can mix together ingredients, or use pureed vegetables, to print food such as quiche, hamburger patties or corn chips. But 3D food printers are slow, depositing one thin layer at a time. And they can't create food out of nothing: the food shapes are made from ingredients that were already edible before being transformed by the printer.

## What's cooking?

In the United States, the National Aeronautics and Space Administration (NASA) is developing a 3D printer that can create a pizza. These could be used to feed astronauts on long space missions, preventing food from spoiling. The prototype 3D pizza printer first prints out a layer of dough, which appears on a hot plate inside the printer and begins cooking. The next layer – tomato – is produced using powder, water and oil, and is printed on top of the cooking dough. The cheese, meat or vegetable topping is printed as a final protein layer.

In future, we'd like food printers to be as common in kitchens as microwave ovens are today. They would create whole meals from scratch using the basic building blocks of food, such as proteins. These would be personalised to meet the nutritional needs of individual people. For example, the printer would know if meals had to be low in fat, gluten-free, or made for someone with nut allergies.

## A cool idea

For any foods that can't be printed, an intelligent fridge and pantry could keep your home well stocked.

A fridge of the future could scan its shelves using ultrasound, which is technology that uses sound waves that are higher than a human can hear. Such a fridge could track levels of food and drink, and order more when they run low. It could also track the calories used in meals, and alert you if you have eaten more than you should. Chemical sensors could monitor freshness, and use this information to move older food to the front on movable shelves, or suggest meals to use up soon-to-expire food.

Researchers at CSIRO say that low-cost technology will soon be everywhere in our homes, creating 'an Internet of Things'. We'll say goodbye to single-computer, broadband-connected homes, and hello to a world with lots more devices connected to the internet. There will be many more screens, computers, smart phones and tablets. And more domestic devices will be connected to the internet – not just televisions, energy meters and security monitors, but also washing machines, fridges and even weight scales. This will allow people in the future to control their environment, reduce energy consumption and have greater access to a future world of home help.

# LENDING A METAL HAND

## Robot servants

WOULD YOU TRUST A ROBOT TO CLEAN YOUR ROOM?

Robots are ideally placed to help with future housework, since they can perform repetitive tasks without becoming bored. Since the 1927 film *Metropolis*, robots have lent a helping hand to humans in many science fiction movies, such as *Star Wars, Wall-E* and *Elysium*. The television cartoon series *The Jetsons* featured Rosie the robot maid.

Could robots soon take over the cleaning? Or, will they take over the world?

## Real robots

Metal humans have featured in stories as old as Greek mythology. In 1818, Mary Shelley published her story of Frankenstein, the scientist who created an artificial human. A couple of years later, a science fiction play by Karel Čapek called R.U.R. (Rossum's Universal Robots) first used the word 'robot'. The term was based on the Czech word 'robota', which means forced labour – so developing them in the real world as servants seems appropriate.

Since the early days of space travel in the 1970s, robots have been used as space probes that can land on and explore other planets. For more than 30 years, robots have performed repetitive tasks in car assembly lines. A typical car factory today uses hundreds of robots. In factories, they precisely produce circuit boards for computers and other electronic equipment. The military has used robots that can independently fly, refuel and select targets to attack.

Honda's ASIMO (Advanced Step in Innovative MObility) robot, first unveiled in the year 2000, looks like a short astronaut. It can climb stairs, run, kick a soccer ball, dance, carry a tray of food, and knows to return to a power point if its batteries are running low.

However, the robots found in the home today are only vacuum cleaners or toys. A robot vacuum cleaner shaped like a large discus became available in the 2000s, and more than 10 million have been sold. When vacuuming the floor, these robots sense dirt, navigate around furniture and avoid stairs.

Robots have also served as sophisticated toys and entertainment. A prototype of the world's first companion robot was unveiled by researchers from the Massachusetts Institute of Technology in 2014. Named Jibo, it can tell children bedtime stories, take photos of the family, remind you about appointments and listen if you just need to talk.

Robots have already come into our lives in a small way. But only about one per cent of the world's robots are in Australia. About half 'live' in Asia (mainly in Japan), a third in Europe and most of the rest in North America.

## Robowash

A robot called PR2 is available today that can be taught to fold washing. But it takes half an hour to fold each towel, and costs close to half a million dollars. The home-based robots of the future will be faster, cheaper and more common. They will be like advanced, mobile kitchen appliances – there to help, but hidden when not in use. Future robots will be able to not only vacuum, but also mop, tidy objects away and do the laundry.

These robots will develop by learning your preferences, in the way that the voice-to-text software on a phone gets to know you the more you use it. Robots could also learn from each other by accessing information held in the internet's 'cloud' storage. Researchers have already begun loading information for robots to use onto Amazon's public cloud, including more than one billion photos, 100 million instruction manuals and 100 000 videos, in a database called Robo Brain.

However, robots still have a lot to learn. They can't anticipate the unpredictable nature of human behaviour. They can be large, heavy and painfully slow at household tasks. Their sight is also a problem. Although a camera enables a robot to navigate around the house, you need a more complicated eye to tell the difference between an empty bottle destined for the bin, and a priceless antique vase that needs to be carefully dusted.

## Robots rule

If robots can communicate with each other, teach themselves new things and learn without human help, could they team up and harm the human race? Not according to the famous science fiction writer Isaac Asimov, who came up with the three laws of robotics. These are: (1) a robot may not injure a human being or, through inaction, allow a human being to come to harm; (2) a robot must obey the orders given to it by human beings, except where such orders would conflict with the first law; and (3) a robot must protect its own existence as long as such protection does not conflict with the first or second law.

Asimov's laws haven't stopped other science fiction writers from creating stories where robots go crazy and threaten the existence of humans. This is the premise behind *I-Robot, Terminator*, and *2001: A Space Odyssey*. And because robots are being used more and more by the military, the idea that they can't hurt a human seems destined only to exist in fiction.

A scary idea is the possibility of computers with artificial intelligence becoming smarter than humans. This point in the future is called the 'singularity'. After this point, it is impossible to predict or understand what such 'intelligent' beings would do. Perhaps they would compete with us for resources, or decide we were too harmful for the environment and exterminate us. Combining future advances in robotics with advances in genetic engineering and nanotechnology could be the stuff of nightmares.

But in the meantime, those robotic vacuum cleaners don't look too dangerous.

# HOLOVISION

## Hologram television

You're probably used to watching your TV in a vertical position. That is, the picture is on an upright screen against a wall or on a stand. But imagine if your TV lay flat on a table. And rather than the image being trapped behind glass, a three-dimensional image floated above the screen like a cloud. You could walk around to watch from different angles, and it would look like the characters were in the room with you. Perhaps you could even touch them. This is called a hologram, and we like to think of this type of future television as 'holovision'.

### Ghostly images

'Help me, Obi-Wan Kenobi. You're my only hope.' So said the hologram of Princess Leia in the 1977 film, *Star Wars Episode IV* – one of the most popular movie representations of a hologram. Holograms first appeared 20 years earlier in the film *Forbidden Planet*, and have featured in many films since.

In the real world, a technique called Pepper's ghost has been used to make hologram-like images for centuries. Scientist Giambattista della Porta first used glass and lights to project a ghostly three-dimensional image into a room in the 1500s. The technique was popularised in the 1800s by John Pepper, who made ghosts seemingly appear in London theatres – hence the name 'Pepper's ghost'. Disneyland still uses the technique today. But while they look like holograms, they're not the real thing.

Hungarian engineer Dennis Gabor invented holograms in 1947, and he won the Nobel Physics Prize in 1971 for his work. The development of lasers in the 1960s enabled holograms to be made more easily. Today, hologram images are common: for example, on credit cards, money and some clothing labels.

But what about moving holographic images? Could holovision – or Holo-TV – take television to a new dimension?

### How's a hologram happen?

A hologram is similar to a music recording, which captures soundwaves from a source of sound vibrations. The sound waves are then replayed later in the absence of the original vibrating source. But instead of sound waves, holograms are made of light. The hologram is recorded by capturing the light that is given off, or emitted, by an object. Later, the light is re-emitted in the absence of the original object to produce the hologram.

To record a hologram, a beam of laser light is split in two. One beam lights up an object and captures an image of it on holographic film. The other beam shines directly onto the holographic film. This creates a sort of code called an interference pattern. When our eyes see this pattern, our brain interprets the code to see every part of the object – even though it isn't actually there anymore.

While 3D TV has been made possible using special glasses, capturing holographic moving pictures is more difficult. However, experts say that a Holo-TV could be available within a few years. Researchers at the Massachusetts Institute of Technology in the United States have developed a cheap colour holographic video projector. It can project holographic video in front of a screen of any size. No special glasses are required, and everyone in the room can see the same thing. The lounge room of the future could soon feature large-screen Holo-TVs – and the classroom of the future could feature holograms of teachers delivering pre-recorded lessons!

And that's not all. Using technology known as haptic holography, information can be linked to the images to provide feedback about force to a joystick. This will allow you to feel the hologram's shape. So in the not-too-distant future, you may be able to touch and even control a movie floating above your Holo-TV, not just sit there watching it.

## A touching experience

Another invention could let you turn up the volume of your Holo-TV by swiping your hand up the armrest of your couch as though it was a smart phone's touchscreen.

Researchers at Carnegie Mellon University in the United States can turn any surface into a touchscreen. Their OmniTouch technology tracks your fingers as you swipe them across everyday surfaces such as a piece of paper, a couch, the wall, or even your own hand or leg.

The invention uses a camera on the ceiling to sense hand gestures, and a projector to transmit images onto any surface. Then all you need to do is rub the arm of your couch to draw a TV remote control, and delete it when you've finished watching. You'd never lose the remote control again!

# A LADDER TO SPACE

## Space elevator

WOULD YOU TAKE A TRIP ON A SPACE ELEVATOR?

**When the Kingdom Tower in Jeddah, Saudi Arabia, is completed, it will be the world's tallest building. According to the designs, it will be one kilometre high.**

Such a massively high building needs massively high elevators. Step in to the lift at ground level and press the button marked '200'. The ride up to the 200th floor will be at speeds of up to 36 kilometres per hour, and the ear-popping journey will take just a minute or so. The Kingdom Tower will have 65 lifts, hauled up by super-strong, lightweight cables made of carbon fibre.

If a building's elevator can lift you one kilometre above the ground, then could similar technology take us into space?

## Russian into space

Born in 1857, Konstantin Tsiolkovsky is called the Russian father of rocketry. In 1895, he suggested that one day people could reach space from a tower reaching from Earth's surface to the height of 'geostationary orbit'. This is almost 36 000 kilometres above the ground. An object in geostationary orbit will stay in place above a fixed position on the ground, rotating once per day above Earth as the planet spins. Think of this as like tying a weight to a rope and spinning it at waist level as you turn around in circles.

Konstantin was fascinated by space travel and rocket science. Having 17 brothers and sisters may also have given him reasons to think about escaping Earth!

More than a century later, the International Academy of Astronautics wrote a 350-page book on Konstantin's idea. The book is called *Space Elevators: An Assessment of the Technological Feasibility and the Way Forward*. The authors concluded that an elevator to space is indeed possible.

Here's how the space elevator would work. A long ribbon would be anchored to a platform floating on the ocean, somewhere near the equator. The ribbon would be made of carbon nanotubes, which are tiny cylinders that are light, flexible and far stronger than steel. Because the carbon nanotubes are so strong and light, the ribbon would be just a few centimetres wide and nearly paper thin.

When we say the ribbon would be long, we mean it. It would need to reach a quarter of the way to the Moon – making it 100 000 kilometres long. The other end of the ribbon would be attached to a counterweight in space known as an 'apex anchor'. As the counterweight orbits Earth at great speed, the ribbon is kept taut.

A rocket launcher would shoot the ribbon into space. But where would the counterweight come from? One scientist came up with a novel idea: find an asteroid somewhere in space, lasso it and use it as the counterweight.

## Up and running

But why bother with all this? Cost, for one thing. Today, if you want to get something into space, such as a telecommunication satellite, the charge is up to $40 000 per kilogram. A space elevator would reduce this to well under $1000 per kilogram.

The Academy of Astronautics calculates that the elevator will be able to carry up to 126 tonnes at one time. That's a lot of satellites.

The space elevator could also be used as a cheap way of exploring our solar system. It could lift spaceships into orbit before launch, slashing the amount of money spent on fuel. This could mark the end of ground-based rocket launches, which are dangerous as well as hugely expensive. Most of a rocket's fuel is used in breaking free of Earth's gravity; so if you didn't have to do that, you would use a lot less fuel.

Powerful robots that could haul themselves up the ribbon would do the elevator lifting. Lasers fired at the robots from the ground would provide their power.

The robots are expected to lift at a rate five times faster than the lifts planned for Saudi Arabia's Kingdom Tower. At around 190 kilometres per hour, you could be in space within hours if you travelled by space elevator.

But the space elevator would face many dangers, including storms and sabotage (people damaging it on purpose). Although the carbon nanotubes making up the ribbon are strong, they are not unbreakable. Space debris, or 'junk', is another threat. Millions of pieces of space junk, which can be natural or human-created objects, orbit Earth. They range in size from tiny paint flecks to old satellites, and can travel at speeds up to 28 000 kilometres per hour.

The United States Government tracks objects larger than 10 centimetres. But the space elevator would need to steer clear of all objects larger than one centimetre to avoid damage.

Then there's the cost. Building the space elevator will probably cost at least $10 billion. However, the space shuttle program has cost twice that, with each flight so far costing $500 million.

## Plans for 2050

The Japanese construction company Obayashi has announced plans to have a space elevator operating by the year 2050. In their design, 90-tonne robot climbers will carry 30 people up the elevator. Their plans also include a 400-metre diameter floating Earth Port and an 11 000-tonne counterweight whizzing around in space.

Don't start saving for the cost of a ticket quite yet. A major challenge is making nanotubes that are long enough. The best we can do so far is just three centimetres – a long way short of the 100 000 kilometres needed. Not to be put off, Obayashi says that 'current technology levels are not yet sufficient to realise the concept, but our plan is realistic, and is a stepping stone toward the construction of the space elevator'.

# BACKSEAT DRIVER

## Driverless cars

WOULD YOU LIKE TO BE DRIVEN TO SCHOOL BY A COMPUTER?

A man is driving his campervan along a highway. He switches on cruise control, and then climbs into the back to make a cup of tea. The campervan crashes off the road. The man then sues the campervan company for not explaining that cruise control still requires a driver to steer.

This story is a myth; an urban legend that never happened. But car technology has now developed from mere cruise control – which simply keeps a car at the same speed – to autopilot, which enables a car to drive itself. Will we see them replace normal cars any day soon?

More than a million people die around the world each year in car accidents, and more than nine out of 10 accidents are caused by driver error. Driverless cars could communicate with each other, keeping a safe distance apart while still travelling fast. They would make the roads safer, because computers don't fall asleep or become distracted by mobile phone calls. They could also stop 'road rage' – where people get so angry at other drivers that they cause accidents.

There are already more than a billion cars in the world today, but by 2050, the planet will have an estimated 2.5 billion cars. Imagine the traffic jams! A computer-controlled car could check traffic conditions and find a faster route. It could obtain traffic light information and set the speed to ensure a run of green lights along your entire journey. This would save time and fuel, which would be better for the environment.

## Sit back and relax

Autopilot has been available on aircraft for many years, and robotic drones can fly without a pilot on board. But that has only been possible because up in the air there is less traffic and no surprises such as sharp bends.

Down on the ground, we now have talking maps to direct us along the fastest route. For some time, we've had cruise control, which allows us to set the car to a constant speed. More recently, 'adaptive' cruise control can reduce your speed if a slow-moving car is detected ahead. Lane-assist technology can sound a warning if a car drifts outside its lane. But a driver still needs to keep control of the car in emergencies. Could future technology completely remove the need for a driver?

The United States General Motors car company built an experimental driverless car in the 1950s. The Firebird III car followed an electrical cable that was buried in the road, and a similar driverless car used magnets in the road. But this technology would have needed entire road networks to be built specially for driverless cars.

In the 1980s, German researchers equipped a car with video cameras and computers. It could be programmed to follow a road, but it could not respond to any changed conditions or an emergency.

In 2004 a race for driverless cars was held in the Mojave Desert from California to Nevada in the United States. The result was almost comical: not one of the 15 cars in the race made it even a tenth of the way through the 200-kilometre course. Most of them crashed in the first kilometre.

## Search for a self-drive car

In 2009, Google began experimenting with driverless cars. Google engineer Sebastian Thrun's best friend had died in a car accident at the age of 18. So Sebastian decided to try and save lives by removing the mistakes of drivers.

Google's bubble-shaped, mainly plastic car doesn't have a steering wheel or brake pedal. It uses radar, video cameras and lasers to scan the road ahead. It also uses ultrasound technology (sound waves that are too high pitched for us to hear) to sense everything around it. The information from all this technology is fed into a computer navigation system, which controls the brakes, the speed of the wheels, and the steering. By 2014, Google's prototype driverless cars had safely driven themselves more than one million kilometres. But they are not yet available for widespread use. For example, the Google car has trouble driving in the rain, because its lasers become confused by all the shiny wet surfaces.

In addition to Google, companies more traditionally associated with making cars are working to remove the need for a human driver. Audi, BMW, Ford, Jeep, Lexus, Mercedes, Nissan, Tesla, Toyota and Volvo have all developed driverless cars. Some cars available now can park themselves, but the computers help rather than replace the driver. It's not yet time to remove the steering wheel.

## Does computer crash = car crash?

At this stage, prototype driverless cars are not available for everyone to drive. They have only just been tested in the real world of traffic. Even so, parts of the United States have made it legal to 'drive' driverless cars on roads, while some European countries and Japan will soon legalise them. The South Australian Government announced new laws in early 2015 to allow driverless cars on public roads, and they were trialled on a closed Adelaide highway for the first time in late 2015.

While the image of driverless cars carrying relaxed, happy passengers speeding along a highway very close to each other may be a good view of the future for some people, others are concerned about leaving the driving to a computer.

We get annoyed when our phone freezes or our computer crashes, but our lives don't normally depend on these working properly. With a computer-driven car, the stakes of a computer crashing are a lot higher.

A robotic car may be able to avoid a collision faster than a human driver, but could a robot use human values to make important decisions? For example, a human driver wouldn't swerve to miss a pothole if it meant crashing into a person walking on the footpath. But could a computer weigh up the relative value of a pothole and a person – or any other two objects – and decide which one to avoid?

And if a driverless car had a crash, who would be responsible? Would computer hacking be a problem? It may be that the technology will be ready soon, but the law and society will not.

# WHAT'S ON YOUR MIND?

Mind reading

WOULD YOU LIKE TO KNOW WHAT YOUR FRIENDS ARE REALLY THINKING?

The gothic-style buildings at Duke University in North Carolina, United States, were the perfect setting for one of the world's most extraordinary experiments in psychology – the study of the mind and behaviour. It was the 1930s, and the university's grand towers, arches and ornate spires added a sense of the Middle Ages to the proceedings. What forces were at play here? Was this modern witchcraft?

## Prying into the paranormal

Professor Joseph Rhine was investigating the paranormal. The paranormal refers to the possibility that we have senses beyond vision, hearing, smell, touch and taste. The professor had a strong interest in telepathy: the ability to read another person's thoughts.

A botanist by training, Professor Rhine was one of the first respected scientists to conduct paranormal research in a university laboratory. During his 40-year career at Duke University, the professor investigated ghosts, telepathy and poltergeists. According to a present-day researcher who has examined more than 700 boxes of the professor's archives, he conducted 'a survey of everything weird in the United States during that period'.

In 1934, Professor Rhine invented the term extrasensory perception (ESP) to describe the possible bonus senses that we might all possess.

Despite the often weird, wonderful and wacky nature of his subject matter, the professor applied scientific methods to his work. He endlessly repeated experiments, documenting the results carefully. He introduced small changes to his experiments and studied their effects. He used statistics (a type of mathematics that deals with how certain something is) to carefully analyse his results. And he even experimented on animals, as well as humans.

## Mind reading on the cards

The search for evidence of telepathy involved a pack of 25 cards. Each card had one of five different designs: a circle, a cross, wavy lines, a square or a star.

Professor Rhine sat at a table opposite the person he was testing. He shuffled the cards, drew one out and looked at the design without showing the other person, who then had to guess the card. The professor repeated the test many times. If there were no such thing as mind reading, you would expect the person to correctly guess the card one time in five, just by chance. This is indeed what usually happened.

Hubert Pearce was a young man studying religion at the university. Professor Rhine later wrote that 'a great deal of what we have discovered by way of important ESP relationships came from the work done with him'.

In test after test, Hubert identified more than one card in five. Once, he correctly named 25 cards in a row.

To improve the test, Professor Rhine erected a screen between himself and the student. Instead of shuffling the cards by hand, he used a machine. Taking the experiment even further, he next did the card tests with Hubert sitting in a campus library cubicle 100 metres away. The professor picked cards randomly at set times. In the far room, Hubert wrote down his guess for each card at the same times.

The test was repeated 1850 times – and the results were astonishing. If Hubert was just randomly guessing the cards, you would expect him to be correct one-fifth of the time (a score of 370 matches out of 1850). But, he actually scored 558. The chances of doing this are extraordinarily unlikely – with odds of billions to one.

Scientific results need to be repeatable to be believed. The trouble was that when other researchers in other laboratories ran the same tests, they never found results that were much different from chance. Critics suggested that Professor Rhine's research subjects might be able to get a glimpse of the cards, or see a reflection. Some said that in the right light, you could see through the cards. There is a theory that the professor might have accidentally passed signals to Hubert about the cards. A major problem was that Hubert could never achieve these above-chance results with experimenters other than Professor Rhine.

In the 1980s, another United States researcher, Charles Honorton, conducted a similar experiment. In one room, a 'sender' watched a one-minute video several times. The 'receiver' sat in another room, blindfolded, listening to neutral sounds through headphones. After half an hour, the receiver watched four video clips, including the one that the sender had seen. The receiver then selected the one that they believed the sender had watched.

After 329 sessions with 240 participants, the success rate was 32 per cent. This is significantly higher than the 25 per cent accuracy (that is, one video out of four) that you would expect from chance alone.

Charles even employed a magician to examine the setup. The magician checked to make sure that the receiver and their room were truly isolated from the sender's room, and that there were no hidden 'tricks'.

Is it possible that the receiver's brain was somehow picking up signals from the sender's brain? To this day, there is still much about the brain that we don't understand.

## Musical brainwave

Mind reading is certainly possible – if you have the assistance of specialised brain imaging.

A medical technique called magnetic resonance imaging (MRI) measures changes in blood flow within the brain. When a part of the brain is more active, it needs more oxygen and attracts greater blood flow.

University of Washington scientists thought that nerve cells in the area of the brain that processes sound might respond to different sound frequencies. If that happened, perhaps you could use imaging to work out what music someone is listening to. Volunteers listened to different songs while having their brains scanned by the MRI machine. Sure enough, the scientists were able to identify songs such as *Twinkle, Twinkle, Little Star* from the brain scans.

In a separate study, imaging showed whether people were listening to quick, medium or slow-paced piano music. Brain activity matched the speed of the music. For example, when people listened to music playing at eight notes per second, their brain waves occurred eight times per second.

University of California researchers recorded brain activity in seven patients who were having brain surgery as part of treatment for a condition called epilepsy. During brain surgery, a patient has to be awake, to make sure that the doctors don't accidentally harm any parts of the brain.

The patients in the study read text on a screen during the surgery. First, they read the text aloud while the researchers recorded the pattern of brain nerve cell activity. Then the patients read the text silently to themselves, while the researchers matched the nerve cell activity with the pattern seen while the patient was reading the words aloud. During the surgery, the researchers could link the patients' brain activity patterns with individual words. The recordings weren't perfect, but they could determine which words some of the patients were thinking just from their brain patterns.

## Million dollar readings

Having paranormal powers will do more than allow you to secretly eavesdrop on your friends' thoughts. The powers will instantly turn you into a millionaire. That is, if you can prove it.

James Randi is a former stage magician. He doesn't believe in the paranormal, occult or the supernatural. The Canadian–American magician offers a prize of one million dollars to anyone who can demonstrate such powers under test conditions.

Perhaps you will be the one to invent a way to read minds, and claim the prize!

# COMPUTER-CRANIUM CONNECTION

## Connecting your brain to a computer

Imagine if your computer could read your thoughts. Rather than typing on a keyboard, you could just think the answers to your homework and it would be done. If your brain could connect to a smart phone, you could call someone just by thinking of them. You could download information to learn a different language while asleep or playing sport. Or, your music device could select songs based on how you're feeling.

*HOW WOULD YOU LIKE A COMPUTER TO DO YOUR HOMEWORK FOR YOU?*

*The Six Million Dollar Man*, *Iron Man* and *Robocop* were films that depicted people with computer-assisted body parts, while *The Matrix*, *Avatar* and *Transcendence* had people's brains connected to computers. Is it possible in real life to connect software and hardware to the all-important third component, meatware (that is, humans)?

## Bionic brains

The 1920s discovery that brain activity can be measured as electrical signals set us on the path to connecting with computers. Since the 1990s, bionic ears (called cochlear implants) have been connected to the brain to enable people to hear. And artificial arms and legs have come a long way since Captain Hook's hand in *Peter Pan*: people who have lost limbs can now use thought to control motorised prosthetic (artificial) limbs that are connected to the brain by wires called electrodes.

Software that can convert speech into words on a computer screen has been around for more than a decade. But in the past couple of years, researchers in the Netherlands have developed ways to convert thoughts into words on a computer screen. Using a brain–machine interface (BMI) that can detect different kinds of brain waves, a computer can detect a person's thoughts while they focus on a particular object. At the same time, the person thinks of a certain letter of the alphabet. For example, they might look at a banana and think of the letter 'B'. This builds a kind of code for each letter, so the person can then think of that object to recreate the brain signal for the letter associated with it. It's not as fast as typing, but it's a start.

## The nerve of it

When we think, some of the 100 billion nerve cells in our brains pass electrical signals to other nerve cells. The signals transmit at speeds faster than 400 kilometres an hour.

While they zoom around the brain, some of these signals leak from the nerve cell pathways. The 'leaked' signals can be measured and interpreted by a set of electrodes that sit on the scalp, brain surface or even inserted into the brain. The electrodes form what's called an electroencephalograph, or EEG. The EEG can then send the electrical signals to a BMI.

People can then use a BMI to control artificial limbs. In 2012, surgeons from the University of Pittsburgh in the United States placed two tiny electrodes into the brain of a woman named Jan Scheuermann, who was paralysed from the neck down. The electrodes poked into the surface of Jan's brain by just one millimetre in the area that would normally control right arm and hand movement. Two days later, the doctors connected a computer to the ends of the two electrodes that poked out from Jan's skull. They could actually see her brain's neurons firing on the computer screen when she thought about

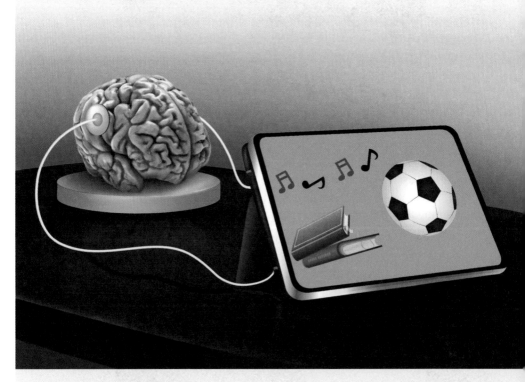

closing her hand. Within a week, Jan could use her thoughts to move a robotic arm left and right, and up and down. After three months of practice, she could bend the robotic arm's wrist to grip objects.

Scientists say that it might even be possible to combine brain control with a device that directly makes muscles work, which could restore movement of a person's own limbs instead of using artificial limbs. Or, signals from the brain's nerve cells could be used to control computers. This could improve the movement of people with disabilities: for example, Japanese researchers hope to soon develop a robotic wheelchair that can be controlled just by thinking.

As well as receiving messages from the brain, BMIs can also send electrical signals into the brain from outside the body. For example, a bionic ear captures sounds, decodes the signal and sends a pattern of electrical currents through wires in the inner ear. The electrical current stimulates the nerve fibres that send messages from the ear to the brain. In a similar way, experimental bionic eyes can radio images from a tiny camera to a tiny computer in the lens of a person's eye. This sends the image through wires to the retina, which is a light-sensitive layer of cells at the back of the eye. The retina then passes the image to the brain.

## Are you thinking what I'm thinking?

Sending thoughts straight from one person's brain to another is common in the science fiction world, and is known as telepathy. In the real world, if we can control computers using our thoughts, and computers can feed signals into a person's brain, then linking these two processes could allow one person to send their thoughts to another person. Such brain-to-brain communication without the need for words would be computer-assisted telepathy.

In 2013, scientists at Harvard Medical School in the United States created a brain-to-brain interface that enabled a person to move a rat's tail just by thinking about the tail moving. In the same year, a researcher at the University of Washington, also in the United States, moved a colleague's hand by sending a brain signal to him over the internet.

Brain-to-brain communication took a step closer to telepathy in 2014 when a researcher who was connected to a BMI in India sent thoughts to a person in France. The BMI in India translated the sender's thoughts into a code of ones and zeroes, which were transmitted over the internet and received by a machine in France. Instead of using electrodes poking into the brain, the French machine used magnetism to activate the receiving person's brain. The received code was then decoded so the second person could understand the words.

Researchers in Japan and the United States have also used magnetism to capture a person's thoughts and turn these into pictures. This is called visualisation. The visualisation of electrical signals could one day allow us to 'see' the dreams of sleeping people.

# CHATTING TO CHIMPS

## Talking to animals

WOULDN'T IT BE GREAT IF YOUR PET COULD TALK BACK TO YOU?

Coco the cat leaps onto your lap.
She purrs and gazes longingly into your eyes.
'Dinner time?' you ask. 'Yes,' rasps Coco.
'Give me fish.'

That would make you sit up and pay attention. A talking cat!
Imagine how many YouTube hits it would be worth.

About 600 000 years ago, our ancestors made complex tools and hunted dangerous animals. But even though they had a voice box, they had no speech. Even primitive speech would have been helpful for these activities.

Speaking is central to human communication. Speech itself probably arose from hand signals and gestures, and only appeared about 50 000 years ago. Human babies communicate using different gestures long before they can say words.

## The language gene

Researchers studying chimpanzees identified 31 different forearm, hand, wrist or finger movements that the animals used to communicate with one another. There are also 18 facial or vocal signals. For example, a chimp stretching out an arm, palm upwards, may be begging for food or asking for help.

So why can we talk, while chimpanzees cannot? The answer lies within us. We have a gene that allows us to understand language. Genes are found in every cell in our body, and hold the information that makes us who we are. Our language gene differs from that of chimps by the tiniest amount – less than 1 per cent.

Our all-important language gene is known as *FOXP2*. It gives us much better control than chimps have over the many muscles involved in making sounds. *FOXP2* probably helps the brain coordinate all the steps involved in speaking. This includes controlling our lungs, larynx (voice box), tongue and lips.

When scientists inserted the *FOXP2* language gene into a mouse, they discovered that its squeak sounded different from normal mice. It wasn't a talking mouse, but it showed the importance of this language gene.

## Bird brain

Many animals have a language gene that is similar to ours. Birds create complex songs, and some – such as parrots – really can talk. But they just copy what they hear; they are not engaging in a conversation. Parakeets, budgies, cockatiels and lyrebirds can also mimic voices.

Alex the African Grey was the world's most famous talking parrot. Dr Irene Pepperberg bought him from a Chicago pet shop, and spent up to eight hours a day training him to identify objects and repeat words. She says that Alex had the intelligence of a five-year-old child. He could count up to six objects placed on a tray in front of him, and could tell the difference between colours and shapes. He knew the names of 50 objects and could describe their shapes and what they were made from. In total, Alex could say 150 words, and even understand the meaning of 'bigger', 'smaller' and 'different'.

Did Alex understand what he was saying? 'Yes,' says Irene. 'If Alex said "Want grape" and you gave him a bit of banana, he'd spit it right back at you and repeat insistently, "Want grape". And he wouldn't stop till he got what he wanted.'

Irene came home one day to discover that he had chewed up an important document. 'How could you do such a thing?' she shrieked. Alex looked guilty, stared straight into her eyes and said, 'I'm sorry... I'm sorry'.

Irene says that she had never taught him these words. She did recall that she had once yelled at Alex after he knocked over a cup of coffee. Upset at her outburst, she had apologised.

Alex died in 2007 at the age of 31.

## Dogs and dolphins

There has been much research into ways in which prairie dogs communicate with each other. Prairie dogs, or burrowing Northern American squirrels, are social animals that live in colonies. When threatened, they make alarm calls. The calls identify the type of threatening animal and include information about its size, shape and colour.

Of course, unlike Alex the parrot, we can't directly understand prairie dog language. But what about a computer translator that can turn animal talk into people talk?

The Wild Dolphin Project, in Florida in the United States, has trialled a new dolphin translator. The Cetacean Hearing and Telemetry project, or CHAT, is an underwater system with microphones and speakers. Project Director,

Dr Denise Herzing, and her team invented a sound and taught the dolphins to associate that sound with a type of seaweed called sargassum.

While swimming with a dolphin pod, Denise clearly heard through the speakers one of the animals say, 'sargassum'. The translator computer had detected and translated a live dolphin whistle for the first time.

Decades of research says that true two-way speaking with animals, even with computer help, won't happen. After all, computers can barely translate text from one language to another, let alone convert cat chat.

# TAKE A TRIP THROUGH TIME

## Time travel

Travelling through time would be a great way to get rich. You could go well into the future, find out which inventions were going to change the world, and then return to the present day and buy the company that invents them. Or, you could go just one day into the future, find out the winning lotto numbers, and come back to buy a ticket.

**WOULD YOU TAKE A SELFIE WITH A DINOSAUR?**

## A time machine dream

Time travellers in science fiction stories have used time machines to visit their ancestors, hunt dinosaurs, and even change the course of history. The first story about a time machine was published in the 1880s, but it was H.G. Wells' *The Time Machine*, written in 1895, that really started people thinking about travelling through time. Today, some of the world's top scientists still debate the possibilities of time travel. Could it ever happen?

## Back and forward

There are ways to travel into the future, but that doesn't mean you'll be able to come back again. To imagine how to travel into the future, you need to know that things travelling at high speeds age more slowly than things that don't move. This is due to the relationship between space, motion and time, which the scientist Albert Einstein discovered.

The theory goes like this. If you could travel into space at close to the speed of light, then time would slow down. When you came back to Earth, you would have aged less than the friends you left behind, so you would now be younger than them.

But, nobody has come up with a way to travel back in time. Travelling faster than the speed of light would make things appear to move backwards, but it's impossible to travel faster than light.

In any case, travelling back in time causes problems known as 'paradoxes'. Paradoxes are things that can't happen and that make your brain hurt thinking about them. For example, if you travelled back in time and prevented your grandmother meeting your grandfather, she couldn't give birth to your mother, and so you would never have been born. Which means you couldn't have prevented your grandmother meeting your grandfather, so your mother WAS born, so you COULD go back in time, so . . . is your brain hurting yet?

## Waiting for the worm to turn

Scientists called theoretical physicists spend their time developing theories on how to travel through time. One theory is to use shortcuts through the universe known as 'wormholes', which are like time tunnels.

The idea is that a time traveller could enter a wormhole near Earth and appear on the other side of the universe, effectively travelling through space and time. Theoretical physicists say that there could be ways of moving the entrances and exits to the wormhole, so that a time traveller could come back to their place of departure before they left. The problem is, these wormholes are usually parts of black holes. Because black holes would squash any person interested in trying to enter them, travelling through time in one is just a theory.

Another way to travel through time is to scrunch up the space in front of you and stretch out the space behind you, effectively bringing the stars closer. Don't worry about trying this. It will take more energy than exists in the entire universe, so it's just another theory.

## Time to get real

Although scientists have come up with ideas about how time travel is possible in theory, and how paradoxes can be solved, there is still a long way between theory and practice. But you never know: only 30 years before people travelled to the Moon, scientists thought the amount of fuel needed would make the journey impossible.

The main piece of evidence that suggests we'll never get to travel in time is that if humans DID ever find out how to travel back in time, then surely they would visit us. So where are all the time travellers from the future?

We do suggest one easy way to travel through time. Simply catch a flight to a country in another time zone – and if you cross the date line, you might arrive before you've left!

# DON'T FORGET YOUR MEDICINE

## Brain pills

**CAN YOU MAKE YOURSELF SMARTER BY POPPING A PILL?**

No more school, no more studying, no more homework. Would you like to learn Chinese? Take this tablet. Want to be a maths whiz? Here's a pill.

If you are struggling to remember all that information, swallow a memory capsule – a brain pill.

## Can fish oil make you smarter?

Omega-3 is a type of fat found in fish oil, walnuts and green vegetables. In the 1980s, omega-3 pills were popular. People thought that they were good for your health in many ways.

One theory was that Japanese people were happier than German people because Japanese people ate more fish, and therefore more omega-3. In 2006, a United States psychiatrist (a doctor who treats disorders of the mind) advised that eating more fishy oils should be encouraged, because it lowered violence and murder rates. People claimed that omega-3 would help your heart, protect you from cancer and stop depression. And some thought it would even boost your brainpower.

Today we know that omega-3 fatty acids *are* helpful. They are important for blood clotting, which stops you bleeding too much when you cut yourself, and for blood vessels to work properly. They are also important in the brain development of babies before they are born. However, international research has found no evidence that omega-3 boosts brain power in children or adults. It doesn't lower murder rates, either.

## Fruit, chocolate and red wine

So if omega-3 doesn't work, is there anything else we could use to make a brain pill? The answer might be an ingredient of strawberries, blueberries and blackcurrants. Known as flavonoids, these chemicals are also found in chocolate, green tea, red apples and red wine. Flavonoids may help memory and learning, and also help your brain process information. They may also improve decision-making and maths ability, as well as lift your skills at physical activities, such as sport. If that's not enough, flavonoids may help keep older people alert, and could protect against disorders such as Alzheimer's and Parkinson's, which are two diseases that can affect people as they age.

A French study of more than 1600 people found that about 15 blueberries, a quarter of a cup of orange juice and half a cup of tofu gave the best scores in tasks such as solving simple maths problems and remembering objects. But it doesn't seem to matter which foods the flavonoids come from – they are all good for you.

Flavonoids may also help the brain's nerve linkages to work. They improve blood flow to the brain and might even prompt the growth of new nerve cells. Plus, they raise the levels of a protein known to be important for learning and memory.

## Develop your brainpower

Computer 'brain training' games have been developed, but these are probably useless. By playing them, you can get better at them – your game score rises – but it won't help you in the real world.

But learning to play a musical instrument does seem to build your brain. It can help you with speech, memory, attention and intelligence ratings. The earlier you start, the better: musicians who began learning before they turned seven have a thicker nerve link between the left and right sides of their brain. Musicians are better at remembering lists of spoken words, and children who study music know more words and read better than those who do not.

Is piano practice painful? Trumpet training too taxing? Why not stick electrodes on your head, instead? Current thinking is that current could help thinking! Neuroscientists have helped improve patients' attention spans by passing tiny electrical currents through their brains.

Dr Roi Cohen Kadosh, from Oxford University in England, has found a spot just above the right ear where electrical pulses improve mathematical ability. Amazingly, the improvement lasted for at least six months after the experiment.

But if you don't fancy the idea of having your head wired, there's an easier way of improving performance. Just turn on a light. Bright lights help improve reaction times and ability in logic, maths and perception. Blue light, particularly, activates the part of the brain responsible for alertness.

So until a brain pill becomes available, we suggest that you eat plenty of fresh fruit and a little bit of dark chocolate. Oh, and avoid studying in the dark.

# HARD TO CRACK

## Exoskeletons

WOULD YOU LIKE A SUPER-STRONG REINFORCED ARM TO HELP LIFT YOUR SCHOOLBAG?

Endoskeletons – who needs them? Having our skeleton on the inside means that our soft skin on the outside is vulnerable to damage. Animals with exoskeletons, such as cockroaches, crabs and crickets, are much tougher. You never see a lobster with a paper cut.

With our hard bones on the inside, is it possible to wear an artificial exoskeleton as protective armour, giving us superhuman strength and protection? This will be possible in the future world of powered exoskeletons – mechanical suits that people can wear.

Even though it sounds like science fiction, this is becoming science fact. The United States military has even asked Hollywood's special effects teams, who built suits for the movies *Robocop* and *Iron Man*, for advice on exoskeleton design.

### Hard shell a hard sell

Powered exoskeletons use mechanical joints, cables and hydraulics (fluid-powered machinery) controlled by computer processors to imitate the actions of the human body.

The first prototype powered exoskeleton was the Hardiman exoskeleton. Built in 1965 by General Electric, it weighed more than half a tonne and its movements were so unpredictable that it was never tried by a person.

Cutting-edge computing, advanced electronics and new materials have improved exoskeleton research in recent years. They are becoming lighter and easier to wear. In the 2000s, Berkeley University in California developed an exoskeleton that enabled the wearer to carry an extra 100 kilograms – the weight of a large person. They call it the Human Universal Load Carrier – or 'HULC' (like the incredible superhero) for short.

The company Lockheed Martin has developed exoskeletons for military use. Like the armour worn by the superhero Iron Man, exoskeletons provide soldiers with protection, extra strength and endurance. Add to this armour some night-vision goggles, GPS navigation and advanced weapons, and you have a daunting warrior. The enemy probably wouldn't stick around to fight if they saw a troop of invincible super soldiers leaping over 10-metre-high walls towards them.

The problem lies in powering this superpower. To move the heavy exoskeleton, you need power assistance, just as power steering helps a driver turn a car's steering wheel. It is difficult to provide a power supply that is large enough to power an exoskeleton, but also light enough to be carried by a soldier. There's no point running into battle with an extension cord trailing behind you, connected to a power point. So while powered exoskeletons have been trialled by soldiers, they are yet to be used in combat.

Lockheed Martin has also developed an unpowered, lightweight version called Fortis (Latin for 'strength'). The Fortis exoskeleton transfers heavy weight through the hard structure to the ground. This enables the wearer to hold a very heavy object as though it was weightless.

## Beyond the battlefield

Exoskeletons could provide strength and protection for civilian use. Firefighters and emergency services could use exoskeletons to fight fires more easily and to rescue people after a disaster such as an earthquake. Exoskeletons could also provide doctors with robotically assisted arms for precision surgery. A company in Japan has already developed exoskeletons to help elderly or disabled hospital patients. The Daewoo company in South Korea has even fitted their dock workers with exoskeletons that enable them to lift heavy weights with ease.

However, the $150 000 price tag of some of these prototypes puts them out of most people's reach.

In future, some exoskeletons could be made of lightweight materials that are sewn into everyday clothing. They could mimic the actions of bones, muscles and tendons to enable anyone to walk further, run faster and lift heavier objects without fatigue or injury. Or, they could enable paralysed people to use their limbs again.

Other exoskeletons could incorporate a jetpack to enable its wearer to fly. Exoskeletons could be integrated into your body and even be controlled by your thoughts. But this level of development is many years away.

Nonetheless, if we make a robot-assisted giant leap to everyday exoskeletons, it would only be a small mechanical step from there to develop much larger and bulkier machines called 'mechas'. A mecha is a large robotic vehicle containing a cabin in which the driver sits to control giant robotic limbs, the sort of thing used by Emmet in *The Lego Movie*. At the moment, however, mechas only exist in the movies.

# SUPERVISION CONTACT LENSES

## Better eyesight

WHAT WOULD YOU SNEAK A PEEK AT WITH X-RAY VISION?

**Are you bored with seeing the world through human eyes? Would you like to have X-ray vision instead? Or would you prefer the ability to look at something and have information about it flash up in front of you?**

With this invention, you could look at a building and see what's inside with your X-ray vision. You then could check the address, history and anything else about the building using a heads-up display that projected important information over your field of vision.

Imagine gaining these abilities simply by wearing a pair of special contact lenses.

## Hands up for heads-up display

They're bulkier and far more noticeable than contact lenses. But putting on a pair of 'Google glasses' can provide you with information about the world around you projected on a heads-up display.

Google Glass integrates a small camera, projector, microphone and speaker into a pair of glasses. A small display appears in the top right of whatever you are looking at. You can flip through different screens by swiping the display in mid-air in front of you, or by swiping the arm of the glasses near your ear. Google Glass can project a compass and directions on a bushwalk, or take a video and post it on social media. It understands voice commands, so you can ask Google Glass to text a friend, or search for information on the internet for you.

The technology even allows you to look at a stranger's face and identify them. However, that particular trick requires a $3000 app used by police officers. It also pushes the boundaries of privacy.

Google has sold about 8000 trial pairs of glasses to volunteer 'Google explorers' at about $2000 each. Although Google have currently stopped selling the glasses while they develop them further, they say that in the future a pair of smart specs will cost about the same as a smart phone.

## Seeing the future

Having a piece of technology mounted on your head is one thing, but could the science be integrated into contact lenses to be an undetectable part of your face?

Wristbands and other devices are already available that monitor your sleep and exercise to help you manage your health. Now Google and pharmaceutical company Novartis are developing a smart contact lens that could monitor your health. The contact lens has a miniature microchip, a hair-like electronic circuit and a tiny antenna attached to its surface. It can measure the amount of sugar in tears and then transmit the data to a phone. This would help the world's 400 million diabetes sufferers track their blood sugar levels without having to prick their fingers for a blood sample. The 'smart' contact lenses may be available by 2019.

Further into the future, similar contact lens technology could be developed to deliver medicine to the body through your eyes. Smart contact lenses could also monitor other bodily fluids via your eyes to manage a range of diseases. For example, tears contain a chemical that can indicate the presence of various types of cancers.

Similar microchip and circuit technology attached to a contact lens could help people with poor vision. An autofocusing contact lens could identify what you are looking at, then change the shape of your eye's lens to help you focus on the correct distance.

All this technology provides a healthy vision of the future.

## X-ray X-perience

With a tiny computer stuck on your eye, it may be possible to do more than just monitor your health or fine-tune your focus.

Researchers at the University of Michigan in the United States have developed technology that could one day lead to night-vision contact lenses. A one-atom-thick layer of carbon, called graphene, can be applied to a contact lens to detect infrared light when it is too dark to see visible light. The layer of graphene could connect to a tiny electrical circuit on another layer of the lens to display an image. This would enable you to see in the dark without the large night-vision headgear used by the military.

As for Superman-like X-ray vision, even this may one day become available. Visible light waves can't pass through solid walls. But radio waves can. Otherwise, tuning in to a radio – or the TV, or picking up Wi-Fi – would be impossible.

Scientists have used radio waves to track human movement, listen to people breathing and even hear a heartbeat. In this way, the radio waves can 'see' people up to 15 metres away on the other side of brick walls half a metre thick. Although they aren't X-rays, the radio waves could effectively enable X-ray vision. The technology could be used one day in hostage situations.

Perhaps one day the technology could be integrated into Rayban sunglasses to make X-Raybans!

# WHAT WEATHER WOULD YOU WANT?

## Controlling the weather

IF YOU COULD CONTROL THE WEATHER, WOULD YOU CHOOSE SUNSHINE OR RAIN?

**Tomorrow will be fine, with a top temperature of 25 degrees Celsius. The day after will be the same. In fact, it will be fine and 25 degrees Celsius forever! This might get a bit boring after a while, but think of all the advantages of being able to control the weather.**

No more washed-out ball games. Have a swim every day of the week. Invite friends over for a barbeque whenever you like. To keep all the plants happy, it will have to rain sometimes. How about between 2 and 4 o'clock every morning? Strong winds, hurricanes, typhoons, storms and floods – forget about them. We'll just have nice, gentle showers.

## Dancing up a storm

For thousands of years, people have tried to change the weather. Ancient Egyptians decorated themselves with green plants and danced in circles, pouring water in the hope that it would rain. In America, Sioux Indians danced around a water jug, threw themselves to the ground, and then drank from the jug. Ancient New Guinea stories claimed that grass carried in a rain dance would pierce the eye of the Sun, making it weep and disappear behind clouds. Unfortunately, none of these rain dances worked. Any rain that came after a dance was just a coincidence – it would have fallen anyway.

Imagine if we could build a giant weather machine powered by energy from the Sun. Each country would be able to program the machine to bring them just the weather they wanted. If a tropical cyclone looked like moving too close to a city, the Weather Minister would press a button to send it back out to sea. The weather machine would be programmed to divert all lightning to strike a series of super-energising electrical poles that would provide extra power. This would also prevent the 100 lightning strikes that hit the planet every second from doing any damage.

## From little seeds, big things grow

There is one method we can use to control the weather just a little. It's called cloud seeding.

Within clouds, air currents and gravity move water droplets and ice particles up and down. These droplets and particles are tiny – only fractions of a millimetre across. It can take a million cloud droplets to form one rain drop that's heavy enough to fall.

Cloud seeding involves flying a plane through clouds while dropping tiny crystals of a chemical called silver iodide into them. Ice gathers on the crystals and begins to grow. When the ice particles are big enough, they melt and fall to the ground as rain. Sometimes scientists use 'dry ice', which is frozen, solid carbon dioxide, to seed the clouds. Again, this helps to make ice crystals form.

Cloud seeding only works sometimes. To start with, you need to have clouds in the sky. Cumulonimbus clouds work well; they are the ones that look big and woolly. You often see them during thunderstorms. Fifty years of experiments have shown that seeding works best with clouds that are rising as they pass over mountains.

Scientists have been able to use cloud seeding in some countries to make more rain fall into water reservoirs such as lakes and dams.

## Fired up for rain

Hail can do a lot of damage to crops. One attempt to control the weather by stopping hail from falling dates back to the 1500s in Europe. When a storm began, people would ring church bells and fire cannons, hoping that the noise would frighten the hail away. In 1896, an Austrian winegrower set up 36 cannons aimed at the sky. On his command, the cannons were fired together. The noise was massive and smoke filled the air. But the hail didn't stop.

A similar experiment was attempted by Queensland's first government meteorologist, Clement Wragge. He wanted to break the drought in outback Queensland in 1902. A set of cannons were fired into the sky over Charleville, in an attempt to entice rain from the passing clouds and break the drought. But the only things that Clement broke were a couple of the cannons, when the large explosions ripped holes through them.

## A change in the weather

All this effort to change the weather over the years, yet so little success. The reason is that the world's weather is driven by massive amounts of energy. We simply can't supply enough energy to deliberately make it hot in Hobart, windy in Warsaw, hailing in Helsinki or rainy in Rome.

Even a single bolt of lightning, for example, can contain enough energy to power a town. And the average tropical cyclone generates 600 000 000 000 000 (six hundred trillion) watts of energy. This is about 200 times the amount of electricity that all the world's power stations could make at once. It's not surprising, then, that there's no way of stopping a tropical cyclone – or even of changing its path.

Humans have influenced the weather, but only accidentally. By burning fossil fuels such as coal and petrol for our energy, we have added massive amounts of carbon dioxide gas to the air. Carbon dioxide and other greenhouse gases trap heat, making the world warmer and changing the climate. But this is not really controlling the weather – it's more like weather out of control!

# COOL WORLD

## Reducing climate change

**All the greenhouse gases we release into the air are changing our climate. Carbon dioxide is the best known of these gases: we create it every time we burn anything that contains carbon.**

Oil, coal, natural gas and petrol are all rich in carbon. They are called fossil fuels because they have taken millions of years to form from ancient plants and animals that decomposed (broke down) while buried underground. Fossil fuels are a major energy source.

## Heat trappers

We burn fossil fuels in power stations, cars, buses, trucks, ships and planes. The result is billions of tonnes of carbon dioxide gas added to the air every year. The problem with this is that carbon dioxide is excellent at trapping heat. Since we began the industrial age in the 1700s, we have pumped an extra 800 billion tonnes of the gas into the air. It's little surprise that levels of carbon dioxide in the atmosphere have risen by more than 40 per cent since then, and are now at their highest levels in more than a million years.

Carbon dioxide isn't the only heat-trapping gas. Methane does the same. This gas mainly comes from mining, natural gas supply, landfill and livestock.

What are all these extra heat-trapping gases doing? Well, trapping heat is the obvious answer. World temperatures have risen on average by almost one degree Celsius over the past hundred years. That doesn't sound like much, but just like your body, the world's climate is finely balanced. Raise your body temperature by a degree or two and you'll be very ill, in bed, sweating.

The global temperature rise causes the climate and weather patterns to change. Many parts of the world are experiencing more extreme weather events – more floods in some places, and more droughts in others. Some places are getting both.

How can the world's population deal with this? We'll need to be inventive. There are two approaches: one is to cut back on the heat-trapping gases in the air, while the second is to prepare for the changes.

## Gas suckers

Moving to renewable energy sources, such as solar, wind, wave and geothermal (natural underground heat) is a sensible step, because these don't involve burning fossil fuels. Planting trees will help, as they suck up and store carbon dioxide.

But many scientists say more drastic action is needed. One idea is to add extra iron to the ocean to grow more phytoplankton. These tiny plants can absorb lots of carbon dioxide. We should be cautious about this approach, though, because the extra iron could upset sensitive ecosystems in the oceans.

There are lots of large-scale engineering ideas to tackle climate change. They're all expensive, and they all have possible downsides. But perhaps a big global problem needs a big global solution. Geo-engineering is one example.

The process of geo-engineering involves large-scale, deliberate changes to the environment. For example, we may be able to mimic volcanic eruptions that blast giant ash clouds high into the air. The ash clouds will act like a mirror, reflecting some of the Sun's rays back into space. That causes cooling, which would counteract all the heat trapping for a while. Or, we could artificially pump a gas called sulfur dioxide high into the stratosphere – perhaps through a massive vertical pipe, or from aircraft or rockets – to cause a similar cooling effect.

Alternatively, we could fire atomised droplets of sea water upwards from 20-metre-high rotors on board massive wind-powered vessels. This could make clouds over the oceans more reflective. A similar idea is to release millions of tiny, hydrogen-filled aluminium balloons, each about four millimetres across. They would float high into the atmosphere and reflect sunlight. The engineer behind this idea calculates that about one million tonnes of balloons would be needed to counteract the global warming caused by humans.

United States scientist, Dr Roger Angel, has published a detailed description of a plan to launch into space a constellation of trillions (thousands of billions) of small screens to form a sunshield. The screens would sit between Earth and the Sun, forming a cylinder-shaped cloud about half as wide as our planet and 10 times longer. Now there's an idea that's truly out of this world!

# DESIGNER BABIES

## Select your child's features

Do you like blue, green or brown eyes? Curly hair or straight hair, blonde or brown? Tall or average height? These aren't questions about yourself or what you like in a friend. They're questions that potential parents could one day be asked about their future baby.

WOULD YOU REALLY WANT TO CHOOSE YOUR BABY?

Genetic research has developed to the stage where the common question today of 'is it a boy or a girl?' could change to be 'would you like a boy or a girl?'

But are humans ready to play God by designing children?

## Would you like dimples with that?

So-called 'test-tube babies' have been born since the 1970s. A woman's egg can be fertilised by a male's sperm outside the body using a technique called in vitro fertilisation (IVF). 'In vitro' is Latin for 'in glass'. The fertilised egg can develop into an embryo (the very early form of a baby). The embryo is then placed in the woman's womb, where the pregnancy continues as normal.

The world's first IVF pregnancy occurred at Monash University in Melbourne in 1973, although the embryo did not survive more than a few days. Louise Brown, born in Manchester, England, in 1978 was the first baby born using IVF technology.

To improve the success of IVF embryos surviving to birth, doctors can check the health of the embryo's genes. Genes contain DNA, which is a code that guides our body's development. In 2013, it became possible to screen the DNA of an IVF embryo before placing it in the mother's womb. This is done to check for genetic disorders, such as Down syndrome and Huntington's disease. However, the technique could also be used to obtain lots of information about what the embryo may look like as a child.

Researchers in the Netherlands have shown that a DNA sample can identify eye and hair colour, and could one day be used to predict facial features such as nose size, cheekbone prominence and the distance between the eyes. This provides the potential to select embryos for appearance.

## Boy or girl?

Unlike selecting the genes that may dictate a child's appearance, choosing a boy or a girl is easy. It is simply a case of identifying whether or not the sperm or embryo has what's called a 'Y chromosome'. Humans have 23 pairs of chromosomes, which are the structures that carry our genes. Females have two X chromosomes, while males have one X and one Y. While an egg can only have an X chromosome, a sperm may contain either an X or a Y. If a sperm with a Y chromosome fertilises the egg, then the baby will be a boy.

Knowing the gender of a baby is important in conditions such as haemophilia, which prevents your blood from clotting, meaning you could bleed to death from a simple cut. Duchenne muscular dystrophy is another example: any sons of a woman carrying a faulty X chromosome will have Duchenne's, which causes the body's muscles to weaken and break down. In this case, the mother could choose to go through IVF and select only the female embryos to place in her womb, since girls cannot have the condition.

However, the ability to select a boy or girl for medical reasons opens the door to do so for non-medical reasons – such as just because you think you'd like a baby girl. This is against the law in Europe and Australia, but in the United States and some other countries, parents can pay to select the sex of their baby.

## One small step for genetics, one giant leap for babies

Genetic science progressed rapidly following the mapping of the human 'genome' in 2003. The genome is the total of all the genes that make up a human. It seems that it won't be long before it will be possible for parents to use genetic information about their embryos to select a baby based on the characteristics identified in its DNA. These could include the way the child will look and behave, the likelihood of it having certain diseases, in addition to whether it is a boy or a girl.

For people who want to know about their baby before an embryo is even created, a company in the United States provides a service to predict the outcome of combining DNA from two people before pregnancy occurs. The idea is to ensure the predicted child of two people won't have an increased risk of a genetic disease such as cystic fibrosis, which is passed on to a child if both parents have a particular form of the responsible gene.

The company says they can predict the likelihood of the 'virtual baby' developing cancer and other diseases, and personality characteristics such as mental stability. But they also list eye colour, skin pigmentation, height, breast size and dimples as being covered by the technology in future.

Baby-designing technology doesn't need to stop at simply *selecting* the ideal embryo. It may be scientifically possible one day to genetically engineer a human embryo. People have tinkered with the genes of plants and animals for years; they have already created wheat that is resistant to disease, and cows that produce more milk. Researchers have also injected mice and monkeys with genes to help find cures to human diseases. Although it is against the law at the moment, one day certain genes could be injected into embryos before they are placed in a mother's womb. These genes could lead to the baby – and its future children, and their children – having characteristics such as being better at sports, or more intelligent.

## Nurtured-nature versus nurture

Just because science says something *can* be done, it doesn't mean it *should* be done, even if it can be done legally.

Gender selection could be used for sexist reasons. For example, in some cultures it is preferable to have a son rather than a daughter. This could lead to discrimination (unfair treatment) against females. Other problems include limiting society's gene pool – that is, the range of genes that are available to be combined in future children – and making certain genes extinct.

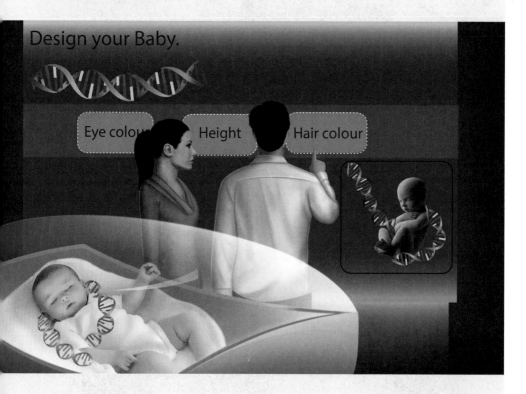

Design your Baby.

Eye colour      Height      Hair colour

Having a parent select the type of child they want would also lead to greater expectations that the child will do what the parent wants. But parents can never know what their child will want to do. It may be that a child designed to be intelligent may prefer a less brain-taxing career, or a baby raised to be an athlete would prefer a desk job.

It may seem unethical (that is, morally wrong) to select for 'desirable' physical characteristics, just because you like, say, blue eyes. But is selecting a gene that favours musical ability much different to sending a child to music lessons? These are some of the issues we need to consider as the science enables us to produce designer babies.

There are also limitations to what a parent could select. Most characteristics are dictated by a complicated interaction between many genes, as well as the environment. In many cases, you couldn't target a single gene for certain characteristics. Also, an embryo's genome may suggest one desirable characteristic alongside many undesirable ones. So finding an embryo with all the characteristics a parent wants may be impossible. You couldn't choose for sure, either: genetics often just suggests the chance of having a particular characteristic, not a certainty. Furthermore, screening or genetic engineering would be too expensive for most people, even if it was legal.

So future parents are still most likely to influence their children's development through nurture – how they bring them up – rather than influencing nature.

# COLONISING MARS

## Establishing a base on Mars

### Schedule

**1 January:** Board flight to launch site

**2–9 January:** Undertake final training and preparation

**10 January:** Board spacecraft for launch

**10 October:** Arrive on Mars

**Accommodation:** Room 17A, Martian Mansions

**Operator:** National Aeronautics and Space Administration (NASA), United States

**Craft type:** Orion capsule, Space launch system

**Journey time:** 273 days

WOULD YOU WANT TO LIVE ON THE RED PLANET?

### Risks

Interplanetary travellers face many risks including, but not limited to:

1. Possibility of explosion of hundreds of tonnes of fuel in the launch rocket. In 1986, the Space Shuttle *Challenger* exploded soon after lift off, killing its seven crew members.
2. Hazards of space travel. In 1970, *Apollo 13* had to return to Earth after an explosion halfway to the Moon.
3. Long exposures to dangerous levels of cosmic radiation that will significantly increase your chances of developing cancer.
4. Possibility of crash landing on the surface of Mars.

### Destination

Fourth planet from the Sun, Mars is the second-smallest planet in our solar system. As Mars orbits the Sun, the distance between them varies from 55 to 401 million kilometres. The gravity on Mars is about one-third of what we experience on Earth, and the atmospheric pressure about one-hundredth.

The surface is a windblown desert with many sand dunes. Bright white frost or ice caps are found at the poles, and are thought to be made of frozen water and solid carbon dioxide.

Powerful winds often create planet-wide dust storms that can last for months, blanketing everything in a dusty, yellow haze.

## Climate

Expect temperatures up to 17 degrees Celsius, with average daily temperatures of minus 33 degrees Celsius. Minimum temperatures at the poles are minus 120 degrees Celsius or less.

Water ice clouds, just like those on Earth, are common.

## Living, breathing and eating

Setting aside the billions of dollars it will cost to send you to Mars, there's the major expense of setting up living quarters on the red planet.

Initially, accommodation would be brought from Earth. But Martian rocks and stones could provide building materials later on. Tunnelling underground would help protect you from dangerous solar radiation and help you escape the unwelcoming surface conditions. And once you have somewhere to stay, you also need to survive. This requires air, water, food and power.

You can't breathe the thin atmosphere of Mars, which consists of carbon dioxide, nitrogen and argon. So you'd need specialised equipment that can get oxygen from carbon dioxide or water.

Mars was once a watery planet, with lakes, rivers and oceans. Today, the scarcity of water means that every drop must be captured and reused – that's EVERY drop, even from urine, sweat and the gas you breathe out.

There is a limit to how much food can be transported from Earth. Soon after settlement, Mars must begin growing its own. Biologists on Earth have researched hydroponics, which is growing food without soil. They hope this can also work on Mars, by using Martian rock and adding fertiliser.

Power will be supplied by solar cells that convert sunlight into electricity. Fuel cells will also generate electricity by making gases react together.

## Could we survive the trip to Mars?

Researchers are already studying the effects on people of the long, lonely journey to and from Mars. Russia and the European Space Agency built an underground test facility in the car park of Moscow's Institute for Medical and Biological Problems.

In 2010, six volunteers squeezed through a small hatch, ready to spend 520 days in a room with an area of just nine metres by nine metres. The crew even had a 20-minute delay during communications with station controllers and family and friends – just like the lag that would occur as radio waves crossed space from Mars to Earth.

When leaving the station, Frenchman Romain Charles announced: 'I'm proud to prove, with my international crewmates, that a human journey to the red planet is feasible.' He and his crewmates, who were called astronots, earned almost $100 000 for undergoing tests to see how their bodies and brains coped during their 'trip'.

The journey might be feasible, but that doesn't make it safe. Many unmanned spacecraft have come to grief on or near Mars.

In 1999, the United States *Mars Climate Orbiter* disappeared on arrival at the red planet. The $125 million craft failed for a very simple reason: the company that programmed the computer's software used imperial (English) units of measurement, while NASA used the metric system. The mistake meant that the thrusters didn't work properly, causing the spacecraft to come too close to the surface and crash.

In the same year, the *Polar Lander* rocket crashed when its landing system failed. Mars also claimed the European mission, *Beagle II*, when it disappeared after landing in 2003 – joining more than 20 American, Canadian and Soviet probes that have been lost on missions to Mars.

In early 2015, European scientists received a small piece of good news when *Beagle II* was spotted on the surface of Mars, just five kilometres from its planned landing place. Unfortunately, they have no way of making contact with it.

## Sign me up

A Dutch company aims to land four people on Mars in 2023. They just need to find $6.5 billion to pay for it. More than 200 000 people applied for a spot on *Mars One*'s one-way journey.

NASA is doubtful that the Dutch plan will work. They say that the technology to set up a human colony on Mars does not yet exist.

# BACK FROM THE DEAD

## Reanimating dead people

WOULD YOU LIKE TO BE BROUGHT BACK TO LIFE IN THE FUTURE?

**We've all heard of horror stories about bringing dead people back to life, zombie movies about the walking dead, and books, such as *Frankenstein*, where mad scientists create living people from dead body parts.**

Coming back to life doesn't have to be a horror story, though. It could well be good news in future if you could be brought back to life after death, especially if you had died while still young due to an accident or illness. You may even want to be frozen until scientists develop a way you can live forever.

## Dead, or dead to the world?

You might have read stories of dead people waking up at their own funeral, but this is because they had been incorrectly pronounced dead. Before modern medical techniques were invented, people whose hearts had stopped beating were thought to be dead. Sometimes they were instead in some sort of very deep, unresponsive sleep, but woke up too late – already in their coffin.

There are different degrees of being dead. People can't be brought back to life after becoming brain dead. This means that your brain and other bodily activities have stopped forever. Ventilators are machines that can keep the lungs breathing, heart pumping and blood flowing even when the brain has died – but these things do not make you 'alive'. If you are brain dead, you have no reflexes, such as blinking when a doctor touches your eyeball. Your pupils no longer shrink when a light is shone into them. It is at this point that family members may decide to switch off the life-support machines.

On the other hand, if your heart stops beating, your blood stops flowing and you stop breathing, you may be clinically dead (that is, according to medical and scientific tests). However, some parts of your body can take several more minutes, hours or even days to stop working. If your brain is still alive, and if you're really lucky, you can be resuscitated (brought back to life). This happens when people with first-aid skills perform CPR (chest compressions and mouth-to-mouth breathing) in an emergency to keep someone alive. People can even remain clinically dead for several hours and still have a chance of being resuscitated. Resuscitation appears like coming back to life; so when a person in this state has recovered, others may believe that they actually came back from the dead.

Machines are even available today that can remove blood from someone whose heart has stopped, add oxygen to the blood, and then circulate it back through the body. They are called extra-corporeal membrane oxygenation (ECMO) machines. An ECMO machine can keep you alive if your heart and lungs fail.

## A cool idea

There's a saying that goes 'nobody's dead until they're warm and dead'. Doctors have found that cooling the human body can help enable a patient to remain a 'bit dead' for some time before coming back to life. This has occurred accidentally, for example, when someone is pulled from a frozen river with no heartbeat, but has been brought back to perfect health when warmed up. It can also be done for people who have had a heart attack, where a clinically dead person's body temperature is lowered in a hospital to bring on a kind of hibernation. This slows the body's metabolism and reduces inflammation (swelling) to increase the odds of recovery.

But CPR, ECMO machines and so-called induced hibernation really only bring people back to life if they have been clinically dead for a few minutes or hours. To come back after many years, you need a method called cryonics.

Cryonics is the process of freezing a person who has just died. Their bodies are kept at temperatures of about minus 200 degrees Celsius until a time when it might be possible to bring them back to life – along with their health and memories. But no technology is available today to bring cryonically frozen people back to life. And only dead people can be treated in this way – freezing a live person is still considered murder.

Many people think Walt Disney, the founder of Disneyland, was cryonically frozen when he died in 1966. In fact, he was cremated, so there's not much chance of him ever coming back. However, a few hundred people have had their body cryonically frozen in the belief that in future they could be thawed out and cured of whatever led to their death.

It would be a bit like travelling through time – but a lot colder!

## Waiting for the right time to return

While it may be some time before humans find a way to come back from the dead, other living things on Earth have found a way to do this. Viruses, for example, can come back to life after thousands of years in hibernation.

In 2014, French scientists managed to revive a virus that had lain dormant (inactive) in Siberian ice for more than 34 000 years. At 1.5 micrometres long – that's just over one-thousandth of a millimetre – it is still invisible to the human eye, but is the world's largest virus. The scientists brought it back to life just by warming it.

So if global warming doesn't make you want to stop climate change, perhaps the threat of giant viruses coming back to life will.

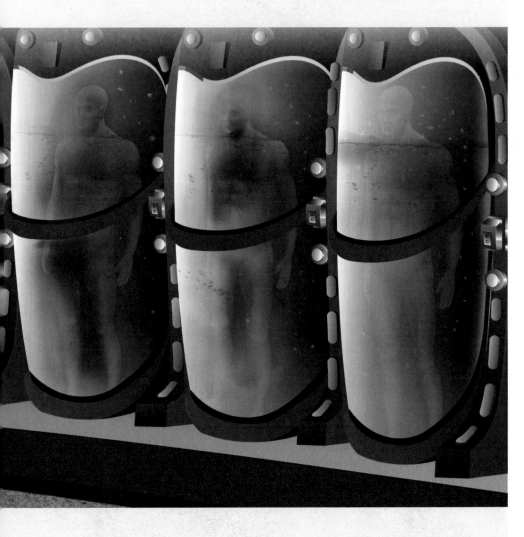

# HOT 2-METHYL-3-FURANTHIOL AND CHIPS

New food flavours

WOULD YOU LIKE CHEMICALS WITH THAT?

Roald Dahl's classic book *Willy Wonka and the Chocolate Factory* included 'three-course-dinner chewing gum'. The gum provided the flavours of tomato soup, roast beef and baked potato, followed by blueberry pie.

Could it really be possible to copy any flavour found in nature?

To make it even more interesting, you could create flavours that don't even exist in nature. Could you make pine-tree-flavoured ice cream, mushroom cordial or yoghurt that tastes like iron? Setting aside the question of why you would want to – unless you're Willy Wonka – the answers are, in order: yes, yes and no.

## Juicy fruit

Many of us are familiar with a flavour that you will never find in nature. Created by the United States Wrigley Company in 1883, it's called Juicy Fruit, and is usually served up as chewing gum. No one is really sure what fruit or fruit mixture Juicy Fruit is supposed to represent. Some people say it tastes like jackfruit, which is a large fruit grown in Asia; others say peach.

To be able to taste a food, it must activate the taste buds on your tongue. The average person has 10 000 taste buds; but their tasting abilities are, well, average. People can usually only distinguish between four or five sensations – sweet, salty, sour, bitter and umami (a savoury flavour).

This is why iron yoghurt can never be. Iron has no taste and no smell.

Natural flavours, such as strawberry, banana and apple, are complex. Dozens or even hundreds of chemicals interact to create the taste and smell of these flavours.

Although natural flavours rely on chemical combinations, often there is one main chemical responsible for the taste and smell. Banana relies on a chemical called isoamyl acetate. It is one of a family of chemicals known as esters, which often have distinctive fruity smells. For pears, the flavour comes from pentyl ethanoate; for pineapples, it is methyl butanoate. And that sweet smell of pentyl butanoate wafting up from the jam on your toast is typical of strawberries.

Over the years, food chemists have worked out the right combination of esters and other chemicals to mimic popular flavours. They have done this by trial and error, and by analysing the chemicals in natural substances.

## Kitchen chemicals

A new discipline known as 'note-by-note' cooking puts chemistry in charge of the kitchen. It involves preparing meals using nothing but chemical reactions.

Pierre Gagnaire is a famous chef who 'cooked' the first ever note-by-note dish in 2009. It consisted of a crispy caramel strip, lemon sorbet and apple jelly. But the dish contained not a trace of real caramel, lemon or apple. Instead, it was made of a carefully selected combination of edible chemicals.

In a laboratory, this approach could create all sorts of oddities, such as a food that tastes like bacon but has the texture of meringue. The chefs say that they're not trying to recreate a chicken or a carrot; instead they are experimenting with dishes that have never been created using traditional ingredients.

## Lab burgers and functional foods

There's a serious side to cooking with chemicals and creating foods in laboratories. Apart from creating new flavours and textures, it offers a new source of food for the world's ever-increasing population.

Scientists at Maastricht University in The Netherlands have made hamburgers from meat grown in their laboratory. Starting with stem cells (cells that can turn into any other cell) from a cow, the team grew 20 000 muscle fibres in small plastic dishes. Then they pressed together the fibres to form a burger. The verdict from a food writer who tasted the very first lab burger was: 'The bite feels like a conventional hamburger. What was conspicuously different was flavour.' In another example, Californian food scientists are working to manufacture chickenless eggs. The product would do away with the need for battery farms with thousands of caged chickens.

Inventions such as chickenless eggs and bacon meringue are an extension of decades of developments in what's called 'functional foods'. Functional foods contain ingredients added to improve health or ward off diseases. Table salt with added iodine is an example. Iodine is a chemical that helps to regulate your metabolism, which is the process your body uses to turn the food you eat into energy and keep you active.

Supermarket shelves are full of vitamin-enriched products. For instance, milk with added vitamin D helps us absorb the calcium in the milk, and reduces the risk of a disease called rickets. This disease causes children's bones to become soft and lose their shape.

Professor James Dale, from Queensland University of Technology, has developed bananas that contain high levels of vitamin A. The fruit normally contains very little of this vitamin, which is important for good vision. The invention is designed to help African children who risk going blind because they don't get enough vitamin A.

## New foods, new noses

Australia's research agency, CSIRO, has come up with a type of sensor device that might help companies develop these new foods. Their 'cybernose biosensors' can detect and measure odours and chemicals in a wide range of substances, including food and drinks. The technology is so sensitive that it can detect just one drop of a particular chemical in a body of water equal to 20 000 Olympic-sized swimming pools.

The biosensors will help food and drink manufacturers create foods with a particular taste and aroma, monitor raw ingredients for freshness and check quality and food safety.

Finally, in case you were wondering about the heading of this story: 2-methyl-3-furanthiol is the chemical that tastes like chicken.

# AROUND THE WORLD IN 80 MINS

## Super-fast transport

COULD YOU TRAVEL AROUND THE WORLD FASTER THAN SUPERMAN?

A plane can get you from Melbourne to London in around 24 hours. Imagine if you could do this trip in just minutes.

## Planes

A commercial jet plane typically cruises at around 910 kilometres per hour. This is Mach 0.85, or 85 per cent of the speed of sound.

In the early 1960s, Britain and France agreed to jointly develop and build a jet-powered 'supersonic' passenger airliner. Supersonic means faster than the speed of sound. Named Concorde, the sleek plane whisked passengers through the skies at more than twice the speed of a commercial jet plane – its maximum cruising speed was 2179 kilometres per hour.

The plane's first flight was in 1969. If you boarded Concorde at 10:00 am in London, you could arrive in New York three hours and 20 minutes later, at 8:00 am local time – seemingly two hours before you had departed.

After financial problems and a terrible crash near Charles de Gaulle airport in Paris in 2000 that killed 113 people, Concorde was taken out of service in 2003. Flying faster than the speed of sound also created noise problems, because the planes caused a bang as they flew overhead. People under Concorde's flight path complained of windows rattling and even roof tiles falling off.

## Trains

The electric-powered French 'TGV' train routinely travels at 320 kilometres per hour. It holds the record for the highest speed recorded by a conventional train – that is, one with wheels running on a track. The train reached 575 kilometres per hour in 2007, travelling from Paris to Strasbourg in the north of France.

Friction is the enemy of speed. The resistance of the track rubbing against the wheels will limit a train's speed. But what if this could be eliminated?

The first magnetic levitation (maglev) system was designed way back in 1907. A maglev train floats a few millimetres above the track, due to magnetic forces in the track and the train repelling each other.

In 1984, Birmingham International airport in England featured a 600-metre-long levitation track that carried passengers at up to 40 kilometres per hour. Since then, things have sped up a lot. Maglev trains in China speed passengers between Shanghai and Pudong airports at more than 400 kilometres per hour. And in April 2015, Japan's JR-Maglev set a world speed record of 603 kilometres per hour.

## Tubes

American engineer Robert Goddard was fascinated by fast travel. In 1926, he launched the first liquid-fuelled rocket. The Goddard Space Flight Center in Maryland, United States, is named in his honour.

Robert drew up plans for rapid transport systems between United States cities. One of his ideas was for a vacuum-train. Trains could speed along an evacuated tube – a tube with all the air taken out – because there is no air resistance to slow it down.

The idea is that engineers create tunnels and then pump out all the air. The tunnels can be on land, under the ocean or even through rock.

Engineers from the Massachusetts Institute of Technology have blasted ping-pong balls through an 800-metre long tube. By removing air from the tube, the balls' speed was doubled; they reached up to 930 kilometres per hour.

United States engineer Daryl Oster has devoted his life to the idea of transporting people and cargo at high speeds through airless tubes. Calling it 'space travel on Earth', he has developed plans for car-sized pods that would float along 1.5-metre-diameter tubes. The pods would be propelled using magnets and superconductors (materials that carry electricity without losing any of it to resistance).

According to Daryl, the system would be cheaper than traditional forms of transportation. He says evacuated tube transport systems can be built for a tenth of the cost of high-speed rail, or a quarter of the cost of a freeway.

## Pipe dreams

So let's combine magnetic levitation and vacuum tube travel. With no friction from tracks and no resistance from the air, transport engineers say that maglev trains in tubes could reach speeds of 6500 kilometres per hour. That would get you from Sydney to London in less than three hours!

Chinese scientists have even built the world's first prototype of an ultra-high-speed vacuum maglev train. They hope that it will reach almost three times the speed of a passenger jet. The test system uses superconductors that produce powerful magnets to lift the train above the track.

Many technological challenges need to be solved before we are racing to school or work through a tube. It would be hard to keep such a large vacuum system in working order, and earthquakes would pose a threat. Plus, it's one thing to travel super quickly; you also need to be able to stop super quickly, and without hurting anyone. So, new brake designs will also be needed.

By the way, travelling around the world in 80 minutes is almost possible right now. The International Space Station moves at 27 600 kilometres per hour – that's more than seven kilometres every second. Astronauts on board orbit Earth in just 92 minutes.

# DESTROYING DIRT

## Self-cleaning materials

COULD WE SAY GOODBYE TO HOUSEHOLD CLEANING CHORES?

**The average Australian spends 26 hours each week on household work. A fair amount of this time is spent cleaning plates and pans, bench tops, windows and floors, as well as washing clothes.**

Women do far more housework than men, according to the Australian Bureau of Statistics. Add up all those hours of polishing, scrubbing and wiping, and women spend around three years of their lives cleaning the house! That's 26 000 hours of often tedious manual labour.

Imagine how good it would be if your house or apartment could just clean itself.

## Clean as a leaf

German biologist, Dr Wilhelm Barthlott, is a pioneer in the field of self-cleaning materials. His inspiration was the sacred lotus, which is a plant that lives in muddy rivers in Asia. Wilhelm noticed that the large green leaves of the lotus plant are always clean and sparkling, as any rain swiftly washes dirt away.

When Wilhelm studied the leaves, he realised that there were two reasons for their cleanliness. First, the leaves have a waxy coating, and wax repels water. Second, the leaf surface is covered with tiny bumps that also repel water. Water droplets sit on top of the bumps, hardly making any contact with the leaf surface. The water easily picks up any dirt on the leaf and rapidly rolls it away.

Wilhelm thought that if he could make surfaces with microscopic raised areas like the lotus leaves, that they might be dirt-resistant, or self-cleaning. He even registered 'Lotus Effect' as a trademark. His first creation was a spoon coated with a rough silicone surface that could pick up a spoonful of honey and then let it drip off. To people's amazement, the spoon was left perfectly clean!

Soon others were applying Wilhelm's invention. One of the first applications was dirt-resistant building paint, which German company STOAG released in 1999. Water and dirt can't bind to the surface, so every time it rains, the paint is washed clean. Some companies have also made coated outdoor tiles. The car-making company Nissan is testing a self-cleaning nanotechnology paint that repels dirt. The paint forms a protective barrier that stops water, oil and other liquids from sticking to the car.

Japanese researchers have made thin, transparent films of a mineral called titanium dioxide, or titania. The films work in the opposite way to lotus leaves – instead of repelling water, they attract water when exposed to light. The water spreads so completely across the surface that it picks up and removes all dirt. Amazingly, the titania film does more than keep itself clean. Sunlight shining on the film causes chemical changes that remove bad smells and harmful bacteria.

The British company Pilkington used a thin, see-through layer of titania to cover glass. They called it 'Activ Glass', and it is widely used for glass roofs and car side mirrors that stay clean.

## Lose the laundry

Self-cleaning fabrics are already coming on the market. The fabric is coated with tiny particles called nanoparticles. The nanoparticles provide bumps similar to those on a lotus leaf, allowing dirt to be easily removed without having to use a washing machine.

Harvard University in Massachusetts in the United States has created a super-slick coating known as SLIPS, which stands for 'slippery liquid-infused porous surfaces'. The team has applied it to two different types of fabric: cotton and polyester. One trial involved coating the fabric with tiny particles of a mineral called silica, while the other used a chemical known as alumina gel. The fabric still felt soft, but water, oil, wine, eggs, mustard and sauce all slipped off without leaving a stain. Messy eaters would be happy to have clothes made of this fabric!

Cleaning marquees (large tents), boat sails and sunshades, which are all made of canvas, is a difficult and expensive task. Self-cleaning canvas could make this job much easier.

You can even buy a spray that makes fabrics repel dirt. A video on YouTube shows chocolate syrup being poured on a pair of treated white sneakers – almost magically, the syrup flows away, leaving the shoes spotless. While the 'NeverWet' nanoparticle spray can deflect chocolate, there are many liquids that it won't repel. So don't sell the washing machine just yet.

# SPACE TOURIST

## Holidays in space

HOW WOULD YOU LIKE TO SPEND YOUR SCHOOL HOLIDAYS IN SPACE?

Looking for a holiday featuring a room with a view – a view of Earth, that is? Or how about an evening walk – in zero gravity? Perhaps you could attend the 2080 Olympics: in space, featuring entirely new sports that make Harry Potter's Quidditch look as exciting as an old-fashioned game of marbles.

These are the possibilities of space tourism. In future, space flights might take off daily and be part of a multibillion dollar industry.

### Star tourists

In April 2001, Dennis Tito became the world's first space tourist. The 60-year old American multimillionaire orbited Earth onboard the International Space Station.

Affordable space tourism took a giant leap for mankind in September 2004, when a spacecraft called *SpaceShipOne* blasted off to more than 100 kilometres above Earth's surface. *SpaceShipOne* cost less than $50 million: just one-fifth of the cost of a single flight on the National Aeronautics and Space Administration (NASA) reusable rocket, known as a space shuttle. The flight was paid for by Microsoft co-founder, Paul Allen. But it was another billionaire – Englishman Richard Branson – who brought flights in *SpaceShipOne* closer to all of us, through a commercial spaceflight company called Virgin Galactic.

Around 700 people, including Hollywood celebrities Tom Hanks, Angelina Jolie, Leonardo DiCaprio, Ashton Kutcher and Demi Moore, have each paid around US$250 000 for a journey to the edge of space on Virgin Galactic's *SpaceShipTwo*. Virgin Galactic had planned their first launch from a spaceport in New Mexico in 2015. But this date was delayed after *SpaceShipTwo* exploded during a test flight in November 2014, killing the pilot. Despite constant delays since the company's first announced launch date back in 2008, NASA has predicted that a seat on space flights may sell for just $20 000 within 20 years.

## Show me the money

Sea cruises around the world were once just for explorers who claimed new lands. Now, anyone with enough money can pay to relax on an ocean-crossing ship. Antarctica was off-limits to all but the most dedicated scientists until just a few years ago. Today, you can even buy travel guidebooks for the icy continent. So once space flights become affordable, what seems like a dream now may be available to everyone with a fair bit of spare cash in the not-so-distant future.

A company called Space Adventures offers commercial flights to the limits of our atmosphere for US$10 000. That will buy you a series of aeroplane flights in which you can experience the floating sensations of zero gravity, due to the U-shaped curve of the flight path. About US$30 000 will get you onto a MIG-25 jet program, which flies to the edge of space. And a suborbital flight – one that goes into space, but below the satellites that orbit our planet – will set you back more than US$100 000. But the true holiday in space, like the one enjoyed by Dennis Tito in 2001 – an eight-day orbital flight to the International Space Station – would cost around US$28 million.

Regardless of the expense, space tourism in the future may not be for everyone. You may think a holiday is more about relaxing by the pool with a good book, rather than gearing up for an intense, adrenaline-pumping spaceship flight. After all, there aren't any beautiful beaches, interesting architecture or gourmet meals to be found up there. There is, however, plenty of space.

## Blast off

Unlike a rocket, Virgin Galactic's *SpaceShipTwo* won't blast off from a launch pad. Instead, it will be carried aloft by a plane the size of a Boeing 737, which can take off from any airport. *SpaceShipTwo* will be released at the upper limits of current aircraft flights, where it will glide for a few seconds before the pilot starts the engines. In the thin upper atmosphere, the sleek spaceship will accelerate quickly to more than three times the speed of sound. Flying straight up, it will reach its furthest point from Earth after only a couple of minutes.

For its fall back through the atmosphere, *SpaceShipTwo* will transform into a larger spacecraft by folding its wings and tails out into a boomerang shape. Like a shuttlecock (the 'ball' used in a game of badminton), air resistance will slow its re-entry as it drifts through the thickening air back down towards Earth. Once it reaches a height where the pilot can fold the spaceship's wings out again, it will change its shape into an aeroplane and glide back to the airport.

## Space to stay

Space hotels are likely to be the next big thing if holiday space flights literally take off. United States hotel owner, Robert Bigelow, has an inflatable space station on his drawing board. The Space Island Group is designing a hotel that will orbit 700 kilometres above Earth. And one optimistic company is even selling real estate on the Moon and on other planets: the Lunar Embassy company will sell you an acre of lunar land for just $20. Of course, they don't really own the land that they claim they are selling to you.

# LIVING THE DREAM - UNDERWATER

## Underwater cities

WOULD YOU WANT TO LIVE UNDERWATER?

**Many people would like a view of the ocean from their bedroom window. How about a view out of your window that's *under* the ocean? While you enjoy the sights, you could breathe in oxygen taken directly from the seawater.**

The oceans are home to the vast majority of Earth's life. But while billions of humans live near the coast, the number of people who live underwater is a grand total of zero. We haven't even managed to map much of the sea floor, or the depths of the ocean beyond the reach of visible light.

Before we can live underwater, we need to at least see what's down there.

People have taken many short trips deep into the ocean using underwater vehicles. In 2013, film-maker James Cameron, director of *Titanic*, dived to Earth's deepest point – the Mariana Trench, 11 kilometres beneath the ocean surface. James made the trip in his *Deepsea Challenger* submarine and stayed down there for three hours. But that doesn't count as living under the sea.

The ocean covers almost three-quarters of Earth's surface. This means the world's seven billion people are clinging to just a quarter of the planet's area. Time to head underwater for a bit of open space – but is it possible?

## Tanks for the place to stay

More than 95 per cent of the underwater world remains unexplored. We know more about the surfaces of the Moon and Mars than we do about the deep-sea floor. Ideas about living on the ocean floor seem about as far-fetched as colonising another planet. So far, they've just been the stuff of science fiction, such as Jules Verne's *20 000 Leagues Under the Sea*, or Hans Christian Andersen's *The Little Mermaid*.

However, just as dreams of living in space became a reality with the construction of the International Space Station in 1998, we have been slowly taking steps towards an underwater city since the middle of the 1900s.

In the 1940s, film-maker and undersea explorer Jacques Cousteau developed a way to dive and breathe underwater. He carried air in a tank called a Self-Contained Underwater Breathing Apparatus, or SCUBA. While scuba-diving is popular for exploring shallow seas, you can only go down about 50 metres. After that, the huge amount of pressure due to the weight of water pushing on you makes it impossible to survive.

The first person to really stay underwater for a long enough time to be considered an 'aquanaut' was Robert Sténuit. In 1962, he spent a whole day and night in a small cylinder 61 metres below the Mediterranean Sea, off the coast of France.

In the early 1960s, Jacques Cousteau led the building of three stations where aquanauts could live underwater for several days. The people stayed in pressurised tanks about the size of a school bus, and even had beds. The best effort involved six people living 100 metres underwater for three weeks in 1965.

The United States Navy developed an underwater living tank called a 'Sealab' in the late 1960s. They had the luxury of beds, showers, fridges, and most importantly: a toilet! A dolphin named Tuffy was trained to deliver supplies to Sealab.

## I want to be under the sea

Research laboratories operating underwater are pretty rare these days. The United States National Oceanic and Atmospheric Administration built the Aquarius lab in the 1980s. Today, up to six aquanauts can live 20 metres below the surface, 15 kilometres off the Florida coast. Nearby is MarineLab, built in 1985. It has become the longest-running place to work on the sea floor.

In Australia, marine scientist Lloyd Godson has spent a week or two at a time living in an underwater home. He built his habitat from old bits of steel and spent 12 days at the bottom of a lake in April 2007. Algae stopped the build-up of carbon dioxide in the air, but Lloyd still found himself sleeping longer hours. He followed this in 2010 by living in an aquarium at LEGOLAND Germany in a tiny underwater house for 14 days, riding an exercise bike to produce electricity.

If you don't think you'd qualify for time in an undersea lab as a marine scientist, instead you can stay at Jules' Undersea Lodge (named after Jules Verne). Located right next door to MarineLab, the luxury hotel in a cabin the size of a small ship sleeps six people about 10 metres underwater. It's hardly a bustling city on the ocean floor housing a deep-sea colony of aquanauts, but it's still a place to live under the sea.

## Breathe easy

Living underwater is one thing, but most efforts have involved breathing air inside a pressurised room. Could we actually breathe underwater, drawing oxygen directly from the seawater – just like a fish?

Fuji Systems in Tokyo, Japan, have developed an artificial gill made of a silicone membrane. The rubbery membrane, called Donkey III, is full of tiny holes that allow gas through, but not water. So oxygen can pass in and carbon dioxide can pass out, allowing a diver to breathe for a short time. In 2002, a diver on television used the Donkey III invention to breathe underwater in a swimming pool for half an hour.

Other inventors have come up with ways to pump oxygen out of the water to produce bubbles that you can breathe in. But nobody has come up with a way for us to breathe underwater long enough to live – so don't hold your breath.

# TAKE OFF

## Self-powered flying

HAVE YOU EVER DREAMED OF FLYING?

**Would you like to fly? We mean really flying, by yourself. Not just showing your boarding pass and sitting in an aisle seat in a big plane.**

You stand outside, look to the sky, maybe flap your arms a bit and jump. Before you know it, people far below are pointing, shouting 'Look … it's a bird … it's a plane … it's … who IS it?'.

You're completely free; able to fly wherever you want, whenever you want. You can soar over cities, above freeways and forests and across water.

## Dreaming of flight

In the 1400s, Italian artist Leonardo da Vinci made detailed drawings of a device that he named an ornithopter. The ornithopter was a machine with wings designed to flap like those of a bird. He also designed a helicopter, to be raised into the air by a spinning propeller (which he also invented). Both craft were to be powered by human muscles.

Leonardo might have been exceptionally bright, but he wasn't exceptionally strong. He would have needed superhuman strength to fly his ornithopter or helicopter. Human muscles are nowhere near powerful enough to enable us to easily flap 'n fly. However, his designs include many of the scientific principles that are used today for building aircraft.

The reason most birds can fly is, of course, that they have feathers and wings. Many bones of adult birds are hollow, giving them lightness along with the strength needed to flap their wings. When a bird glides, it is flying in much the same way as a plane. Unlike a plane, though, birds flap their wings – twisting and folding them.

If you could sprout wings, they would need to be massive to lift your body weight. The wandering albatross, which is just a fraction of the weight of an adult human, has the largest wingspan of any living bird. In 1965, an albatross with a 3.6-metre wingspan was caught in the Tasman Sea between Australia and New Zealand. That span's more than twice as wide as the height of an average person.

Since the late 1990s, people have been dressing in 'wingsuits' and gliding through the air, thanks to the large surface area of the costumes. The flight begins by leaping out of a plane or off a high ledge. Wingsuit pilots can reach speeds of 200 kilometres per hour forward, while they fall towards the ground at 70 kilometres per hour. Speaking of falling, the pilots normally activate a parachute when they get close to the ground.

But wingsuits, like parachutes, involve controlled falling. These adventurous people in their squirrel suits are not engaging in single-person powered flight.

## Backyard ballooning

Californian Larry Walters dreamed 'of going up into the clear blue sky in a weather balloon'. So one day in 1982, he turned a garden chair into his own flying machine by tying 45 weather balloons filled with helium gas to it. Then he strapped himself in.

Soon Larry found himself 5000 metres above the ground, where he was spotted by very surprised aircraft pilots. At this height, conditions were cold, so he burst a couple of the balloons to make the chair go down.

On its way down, the chair became entangled in a power line, blacking out the local area. Luckily, Larry was able to safely climb down to the ground.

Following the 45-minute flight, the Federal Aviation Administration fined Larry for breaking the law. A safety inspector said that, 'if he had a pilot's licence, we'd suspend that. But he doesn't'.

## In a flap

The first human-powered flight was made in England in 1961. Gliding teacher, Derek Piggott, became the first person to take off and fly purely by his own efforts. He piloted and powered a 'flying bicycle' designed by Southampton University. Pedalling furiously, he kept the plane's propeller spinning fast enough to fly for 64 metres at Lasham airfield, just 1.8 metres above the runway.

In 1989, a human-powered helicopter became reality. A team from California Polytechnic State University built one that flew for 7.1 seconds. It rose just a few centimetres. The helicopter was named *da Vinci III* in honour of Leonardo.

The first human-powered flapping-wing craft to keep flying for a reasonable time was the *Snowbird* in 2010. A team from the University of Toronto Institute for Aerospace Studies in Canada designed and built the aircraft. Student Todd Reichert sat in a cockpit hanging beneath the wings and pumped a bar with his feet to make the wings move up and down. *Snowbird* flew 145 metres before gently landing on the grassy test field.

If it's so difficult to power yourself, why not get a little assistance? In the 1960s, Wendell Moore, a New York engineer, invented the Rocket Belt. This is a small jet-powered device that you wear like a backpack. The Rocket Belt is fuelled by nitrogen and a chemical called hydrogen peroxide.

If you're brave enough to press the 'go' button, the extremely hot steam blasting from the bottom of your Rocket Belt will thrust you upwards and onwards for an exciting 20-second flight. If the 100 kilometres per hour speed that you can fly at doesn't impress onlookers, the terrifyingly loud scream of your jet engine will.

# SCIENTISTS HOT ON THE TRAIL OF A COLD CURE

## Cure for the common cold

**The common cold lasts a week. Apply the best known cures, and you'll get rid of it within seven days. So goes the joke.**

A cold is the most common illness in humans. According to Australian health insurance company, Medibank, the amount of sick days adults take from work costs our economy $7 billion each year, because employers have to pay their workers when they are ill. The common cold would have been responsible for many of these sick days, as well as many school days missed by children.

As well as all those lost work and school days, each year people spend billions of dollars on cough and cold medicines. These medicines often include antibiotics, even though they have no effect on colds, which are caused by viruses. Antibiotics are only useful for illnesses caused by bacteria.

Imagine how much a cold cure would be worth. You would stop people getting ill, and save them the money they often spend on products that treat the symptoms, not the cause.

## Cold war

The common cold has no common source. That's part of the problem for researchers who are trying to produce a cure.

Any one of hundreds of different viruses can cause a cold. The culprits come from nearly a dozen different virus families. The rhinovirus family causes up to half of all colds. Then there are the families of coronaviruses, influenza viruses and many others.

When you catch a cold, it begins by virus particles entering your body. They bore holes into the cells in your nose and throat, and then invade the cells and force them to mass-produce new virus particles.

Your body's immune system responds, sending in white blood cells to fight off the virus. Your temperature rises, which helps certain types of immune cells to work better. Proteins in your blood coat the viruses and infected cells, which helps your white cells identify the enemies. Then your body starts making mucus – otherwise known as snot – to trap and get rid of the virus particles. This helps isolate the infection to your nose, stopping the virus from invading other parts of your body.

Your runny nose and high temperature are both signs of the war being waged within you against the viral invaders. By the time you actually feel a cold coming on, you have probably been infected for more than a day.

The search for a cold cure is made even more difficult by the fact that a virus can swiftly change, or mutate, its genes. This helps it to evade any drugs designed to destroy it.

## Locking up the virus shell

In promising research at Oxford University in England, scientists have found a compound that sticks to a virus known as Enterovirus 71. This is one of the viruses that cause the common cold. It also causes polio and hand, foot and mouth disease.

The research team leader, Professor Dave Stuart, says: 'There are no drugs available at all against the whole group of viruses that include the common cold'. So, this new compound could be the first useful treatment. It works by locking up the outer shell of Enterovirus 71, which stops it from opening inside your cells and releasing harmful material. Since it can't open its shell, it can't infect you.

## How to not catch a cold

There's a saying that sometimes the treatment is worse than the cure. Drugs can have bad side effects, such as nausea (vomiting) and diarrhoea, making people really feel unwell. Colds are usually not as bad as these potential side effects, so at the moment it isn't worth the risk trying to fight the infection with medicine.

Prevention is the best cure. Keep away from people with colds as much as possible, and wash your hands regularly with soap and water. Resting and drinking lots of water to keep hydrated will give your immune system the best chance at fighting the infection.

Thousands of years of sniffles have led to a long list of home remedies. Although they aren't supported by real scientific evidence, chicken soup, a cup of tea or steam might help blow out the mucus, while honey or a saltwater gargle might soothe the throat. There's even a theory that hot chilli peppers can ease a stuffy nose.

Finally, cold temperatures don't cause colds. You can easily get a cold on the hottest day in summer. In winter, though, people spend lots of time indoors, which increases your chances of coming into contact with people with a cold. And the more exposure you have to people carrying the virus, the greater the chance of it spreading.

# TWO PLACES AT ONCE

## Teleportation

WOULD YOU LIKE TO TRAVEL BY TELEPORT?

**School starts at 9:00 am. It's 8.59. No rush: you have plenty of time. You stroll over to the teleporter, press the button and ... you're in the classroom, all ready for science class.**

Teleporting would take all the hassle out of commuting.

The *Star Trek* TV series featured a teleporter called a 'transporter'. When Captain Kirk wanted to return to the starship *Enterprise*, he would command his chief engineer: 'Scotty, beam me up'. The transporter would convert the captain and anything with him into an energy pattern, and then beam the pattern to a target. On arrival, the pattern was turned back into matter – and hopefully, Captain Kirk was still in one piece.

### The ups and downs of entanglement

Professor Ronald Hanson from Delft University of Technology in the Netherlands says that nothing in the laws of physics prevents the teleportation of large objects, including humans.

'If you believe we are nothing more than a collection of atoms strung together in a particular way, then in principle it should be possible to teleport ourselves from one place to another,' he says.

While Professor Hanson still needs to commute to work in the traditional way, he and his team have succeeded with teleporting – but only information, not objects.

To do this, they have used a concept known as 'entanglement'. This is an area of physics that the famous scientist Albert Einstein referred to as 'spooky action at a distance'. The tiny particles called electrons that are found in atoms have a characteristic direction of 'spin': either 'up' or 'down'. When two electrons interact, become entangled and are then forced to separate, they take on opposite spins. They are like mirror images of each other.

Here is the interesting part. If you now change the spin of one of the electrons, the second electron immediately reverses its own spin direction, so that it remains as a mirror image of the first one. In other words, if you upset one member of this 'couple', you automatically upset them both!

This close relationship between two entangled particles applies no matter how far apart they are. They can be across a room, across a city or even across a galaxy – if you change the state of the nearby particle, the far entangled mate will instantly respond. Professor Hanson's team has already managed to teleport information encoded into tiny subatomic particles between two points that are metres apart.

If you cause changes to entangled particles repeatedly, or you do it with lots of particles, then you can pass information from one place to another. After all, everything you get via the internet comes to you in binary form – a series of 1s and 0s. But the internet uses wires or wireless radiation (such as radio waves). Teleporting information by entanglement instantly moves it from one place to another without wires or radio waves. The information arrives at its destination without travelling to get there.

There's a world of potential applications for teleporting particles, such as super-fast communication technology and 'quantum' computing. Quantum computers use individual atoms or particles instead of the usual transistors, which are small devices that control the flow of electrical current in normal computers.

## Teleporting a person

Back to you – and the promise of a fast trip to school or, perhaps more desirable, a fast trip home.

It all comes down to numbers. Teleporting data between two electrons is one thing. But your body contains approximately seven billion billion billion atoms. Plus, each one of your atoms contains particles such as protons, neutrons and electrons. Physicists have calculated that to recreate a person from a teleport would involve more than three million billion billion billion billion 'bits'. A bit is the basic unit of computing communication; the electron we talked about earlier as spinning 'up' or 'down' represents just one bit.

You'd also need to be confident that every one of those billions and billions of 'ups' and 'downs' was teleported correctly. A faulty code in a computer program can cause a crash, bringing the computer to a sudden stop. This is not something you'd want to have happen to you, your body, your thoughts, personality and memories. Remember too, the final step of teleportation involves destroying the original. Once you've gone, you've gone forever.

# ENERGY-COLLECTING
## SKIS AND SKATEBOARDS

Power from movement

WOULD YOU LIKE TO POWER YOUR ELECTRICAL GADGETS YOURSELF?

**Have you ever thought about all the energy that's lost as you move around – walking, playing sport, or just picking something up off the floor?**

**The energy you use as you walk up a hill carrying a skateboard is converted to a different form of energy as you speed back down the hill. But some of the effort you put in to get up the hill is lost – it's wasted as heat energy.**

Imagine if that energy could be captured. At the bottom of the hill, the energy could be used to power the wheels to take you and your skateboard up the next hill. Or skiers could speed down a run, collecting and storing energy in their skis. This could be converted into electricity to power a tow to drag them uphill for the next run.

Can this be done – and could the electricity be used to power more than just skateboards and skis?

## The potential of using potential energy

Any object above the ground has the potential to fall due to gravity. Energy that is stored in objects and available to be used is called potential energy. The higher you go, the more gravitational potential energy you gain. As you drop, you lose your potential energy – it is changed into the energy of motion, which is called kinetic energy. Anything that moves has kinetic energy. And as objects move, some of their kinetic energy is turned into other forms of energy, such as heat and noise. It's also possible to turn kinetic energy into useful energy, such as electricity.

Shaking an object can generate three milliwatts of harvestable energy. That's enough energy to power one of those shakeable torches. Walking produces less than one-tenth of this amount of energy (about 200 microwatts; there are

1000 microwatts in a milliwatt), while pulling open a drawer generates just one-hundredth of this amount (30 microwatts).

## Power me up

Plenty of inventions on the market convert kinetic energy into small amounts of electricity.

The Toyota Prius takes the heat energy generated from braking, and changes it into electrical energy to charge the car's battery. The Siemens and XTrapolis trains running on Melbourne's train lines can capture energy through a process called regenerative braking. But this energy isn't used, because the ageing train network is not equipped to make use of it.

CSIRO and other researchers have developed wearable, flexible batteries. Materials that make electricity when they are twisted or pressed can be woven into the fabric used to make clothing. Just by moving around, the wearer can create electricity that is stored in the flexible battery to power a mobile phone or other small electronic device.

Researchers at the Massachusetts Institute of Technology in the United States have made a battery that uses temperature differences to change waste heat into electricity. The battery is charged at about 60 degrees Celsius and generates electricity when it is cooled to 15 degrees Celsius.

Jessica Matthews, a graduate of Harvard University in the United States, developed a soccer ball that generates energy when kicked. The energy can then be used to power devices in areas with limited electricity, such as Jessica's family home in Nigeria. About half an hour of kicking can power a light-emitting diode (LED) lamp for three hours.

Some fitness centres produce electricity by making use of the energy people burn while working out on the gym equipment. Some nightclubs even capture energy as people dance. Materials in the dance floor generate electricity to power appliances such as the air conditioner to cool down all those hard-working people.

## Carnot do it

Could electricity harvested from the energy we generate just by moving around be an alternative energy solution? Can people power our planet?

The answer is no: at least in the foreseeable future.

Researchers who try to increase the amount of electricity generated by capturing heat from kinetic energy can only go so far. At a certain point, they come up against a law of usable electricity, which is called the Carnot limit. In the early 1800s, Frenchman Nicolas Carnot (pronounced car-noh) explained that there was a limit to how much heat energy can be turned into useful energy. This was quite a remarkable observation, seeing that heat wasn't fully understood back then. His concepts are still used today, and state the maximum amount of heat energy that can be converted to electricity.

Back in Nicolas' day, steam engines converted heat into energy with less than a three per cent efficiency. This means that almost all (97 per cent) of the heat was lost instead of being used as energy. Gas-fired steam turbines in power plants today have an efficiency of about 40 per cent. Their Carnot limit – that is, the highest efficiency that can be reached for steam engines – is about 50 per cent. Car engines have heat efficiencies of about 20 per cent, with their Carnot limit being about 37 per cent.

Steam and car engines convert heat energy into work at very high temperatures. At the low temperatures obtained from waste heat, only about two per cent of the heat energy is converted into electricity. The Carnot limit for generators (devices that make electricity) at this temperature would be less than 10 per cent. So while heat and kinetic energy may be able to charge small electronic devices, such as a mobile phone, it won't drag skiers up to the top of a ski run. And it certainly isn't the answer to the world's energy needs.

Nonetheless, computer company IBM has predicted that 'people power' will soon help provide electricity to run our homes, offices and cities simply by moving around. But don't unplug your TV just yet.

# SPEAKING IN MANY TONGUES

## Universal language translator

About 7000 languages are spoken around the world. Many people learn more than one language so that they can communicate more widely. But will this be necessary in the future, if you can instead just talk into a universal language translator that can speak in a foreign language for you?

**HOW WOULD YOU LIKE TO SPEAK TO ANYONE ON THE PLANET?**

In Douglas Adams' science fiction book, *The Hitchhiker's Guide to the Galaxy*, people put a creature called a Babel fish in their ear to understand alien languages. In *Star Trek*, the crew of the *Enterprise* used a universal translator device to have conversations with aliens. Could a device that instantly translates language become available in the real world?

## All around the world

Some people have tried to avoid the need for a universal translator by developing a universal language. About 200 artificial languages have been invented. In the 1880s, Ludwig Zamenhof from Poland introduced the most popular version, which was called Esperanto. Ludwig wanted the easy-to-learn language to catch on around the world and promote peace and understanding. Although it didn't take over the whole world, Esperanto is still spoken today by as many as two million people.

The world's most popular language is Mandarin, which is spoken by more than a billion people. This is followed by, in order: English, Spanish, Hindi, Arabic, Bengali, Russian, Portuguese, Japanese, German and French. But language is a living thing. On our globally connected planet, some languages may merge in the future to evolve into a single, hybrid language. More than three-quarters of the world's English speakers don't speak English as their first language, and non-English words and sounds are now influencing spoken English. Linguists (people who study language) suggest that a single language may emerge that they call 'Panglish', or Pan English.

## Lost in translation

Before we have a universal language, there will be a demand for universal translators.

Early computer-generated translations, called machine translators, were slow and inaccurate. For example, in the mid-1960s, IBM's language translation software took almost one and a half minutes to translate just one second of speech. Its lack of accuracy meant the results weren't really worth waiting for.

Nowadays, numerous websites, apps and calculator-sized computers can convert text from one language into another. The first online machine translators in the 1990s simply substituted words in the original text with the translated word. However, machine translators don't have the human ability to understand the context or situation in which the word is used. This meant the results were far from perfect.

Today's online translators, such as Google Translate and Babylon, use the mathematical techniques of statistics. They compare the text you want translated with text that has previously been translated, to improve the chance of using the right words. The more translations it completes, the better the machine translator is at 'guessing' the context.

While online translators do a good job at translating from one language into another, things get messy in situations where three nationalities join the conversation. For example, when the opening sentence of this paragraph is translated by the translator Babylon into Chinese, then into Spanish, and then back into English, the result is the following nonsensical sentence: *The translation staff to do a good job in the transition from one language to another, it becomes a lot of problems, three people to participate in the conversation.*

Nonetheless, online translators are extremely popular, since they are so easy to use, and can provide you with a 'feel' of the conversation. For example, Google Translate translates enough text every day to fill more than one million books.

## Parlez-vous alien?

Translating text online is one thing. But we've also seen advances in the translation of spoken language. This involves speech recognition, followed by machine translation and then speech generation – all in the blink of an eye.

United States soldiers who were in Iraq in the 2000s used a laptop-based system called IraqComm and a handheld device called the Speechalator. Iraqis could speak Arabic into a microphone, and the speech recognition software would convert their words into text. The Speechalator then translated the words into English and spoke them. The system worked well because it focused on a limited number of words required by soldiers.

Japanese company NEC introduced the world's first real-time language translator on a mobile phone in the late 2000s. The device could convert Japanese phrases commonly used by travellers into English text. Since then, apps have become available to translate text messages between smart phones.

In 2014, Microsoft demonstrated instant voice translation via Skype. It enabled an American to speak in English with someone in Mexico speaking Spanish, instantly translating their conversation. It seems that instant speech translation in a range of languages may not be far away.

But to make universal translators truly universal – that is, working across the universe – they will need to be able to work with alien languages. That way, if the Search for Extraterrestrial Intelligence (SETI) – a United States organisation that looks for life on other planets – ever picks up a message, we'll be ready to translate it.

# ON AND ON AND ON AND ON

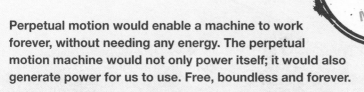

## Perpetual motion

WHAT WOULD YOU POWER WITH A PERPETUAL MOTION MACHINE?

**Perpetual motion would enable a machine to work forever, without needing any energy. The perpetual motion machine would not only power itself; it would also generate power for us to use. Free, boundless and forever.**

There's just one catch: such a machine does not exist, cannot exist and never will exist. It would be good if it did, though. The planet's energy problems would be solved in one easy step.

### Perpetual search for perpetual motion

For centuries, scientists, fraudsters and even fraudulent scientists have been coming up with ideas for perpetual motion machines. You'll find them on the internet. Don't believe them.

Here's one. Imagine a Ferris wheel with the cabins replaced by hanging buckets. The attendant pours water into the buckets as they pass by. When the first full bucket reaches the very top, it hits a horizontal bar that makes the water tip out. The falling water lands in the next empty bucket below. The force of the water falling from the top bucket pushes the lower bucket down, keeping the big wheel rotating. Then the next full bucket reaches the top and drops its load.

The attendant stands back and watches, dreaming of all the money to be made by hooking the ever-turning Ferris wheel axis to a generator and selling the electricity. Dream on.

In the 1500s, a Jesuit priest named Johannes Taisnerius had an exciting idea. Attach a sloping wooden track to a stand. Fix a strong magnet to the top of the stand. Drill a hole in the track near the top. Finally, place an iron ball at the bottom of the track. In Johannes' mind, the magnet would pull the ball up the slope to the hole. The ball would fall through the hole and onto a second track that would take it back to the starting point. Repeat.

The trouble with his design is that a magnet strong enough to draw the ball up the slope would pull it straight over the hole. The ball would stick to the magnet. And so the machine was never built.

In 1870, in New Jersey in the United States, an enterprising man named Paine demonstrated a perpetual 'electromagnetic' machine. This was a powerful device capable of sawing wood using the energy from just four small batteries. Sceptical scientists tried unsuccessfully to find out how it really worked.

It was only after Paine left town that they discovered the secret. There was a hole in the floor, and a belt drive connected the saw to a powerful steam engine below.

## Scientific laws

The quest for getting energy for nothing continues to this day. People have made plans for UFO-like spaceships and hovercraft, 'antigravity' devices, motors that mysteriously run on water and power generators that suck energy from vacuums. Not one has ever worked.

There are laws against perpetual motion machines: the scientific laws of thermodynamics (the relationships between heat and energy). The first law of thermodynamics says that energy can't be created or destroyed. Perpetual motion machines are in trouble with this law, since they seek to create energy from nothing.

The second law of thermodynamics says that heat cannot pass from a cooler to a hotter object. It can only move from a hotter object to a cooler one. In other words, energy – like the water in our imaginary Ferris wheel – can't run uphill.

## Atomic energy

The only serious hope for perpetual energy lies in quantum mechanics. This is the world of the atom and subatomic particles (particles that are smaller than an atom). In 2012, Nobel Prize-winning physicist, Frank Wilczek, decided that 'time crystals' might be possible. Time crystals are arrangements of atoms that will move forever in a repeating pattern.

Physicists at Berkeley University in California are planning to test Frank's idea by building a time crystal. The crystal will consist of a ring of 100 charged calcium atoms (called ions). Wires will be used to create an area called an electric field that will keep the calcium ions to a region roughly the width of a human hair.

Next, the ring of ions will be cooled to around one-billionth of a degree above absolute zero – the lowest possible temperature. Then the researchers will create a magnetic field. If the time crystal theory is right, the ring should start spinning, and continue to do so forever.

It is one thing to (possibly) make 100 atoms spin. But it's completely another thing to generate any useful amounts of energy from this tiny setup. The old saying is true: you can't get something from nothing.

# CASHLESS COMMUNITY

## eMoney replacing coins and banknotes

The contents of a wallet today differ from those of 30 years ago. Back then, it was likely to contain a pile of banknotes and maybe one plastic card with a magnetic strip on the back. Today, it is likely to contain just a few notes and several cards embedded with intelligent chips. Thirty years from now, you probably won't even have a wallet. Instead, you'll buy things with a smart phone, watch or fingerprint.

DO YOU STILL USE REAL MONEY?

## A change from change

Money was first used around 5000 years ago. Before then, people used to trade one item for another. From metal coins, money changed to paper and then plastic banknotes.

Just one generation ago – when your parents were kids – people didn't have access to their money over the weekend. They had to withdraw cash before the banks closed at 4:00 pm on a Friday, and hope they had enough to last until Monday morning. There were no automatic teller machines (ATMs). And, most people didn't have credit cards.

By 2013, cash was used to pay for less than half of our purchases. In 2015, the Reserve Bank (Australia's central bank) said the average Australian went to an ATM about once a week and carried about $55 in cash.

The convenience of new technologies, such as Paywave, means that we are using less and less cash. A pocket full of coins is uncommon these days. There's no need to calculate how much change is required when you buy something digitally. Some researchers predict that in another decade we won't use cash at all.

## Trash the cash

Notes and coins are a physical representation of how much money we have. In the 1980s, David Chaum, a United States computer science graduate, raised the idea of 'digital' money.

Digital money moves the physical representation into the virtual world. Rather than storing and transferring real notes and coins, the money's value can now be stored and transferred digitally, on computers. PayPal, WebMoney and many other companies now enable us to transfer electronic money, or eMoney, around the world using the internet.

We can also store eMoney outside a central banking system using a virtual currency, such as Bitcoin. People can pay each other with Bitcoin without transferring it through a company or bank. Satoshi Nakamoto, an unidentified person rumoured in 2015 to be an Australian, invented Bitcoin in 2008. By 2011, one bitcoin was worth about 25 cents in the real world. The value of one bitcoin increased to more than $1000 in 2014, before dropping in value to a few hundred dollars. Bitcoin is mainly used when buying things online, such as Wordpress and Microsoft software products, but around 5000 bitcoins a day are used in shops.

People used to use credit cards only to buy expensive things, due to the fees that shops need to pay to process the credit card transactions. However, now money can be stored on a smart card or smart phone for small purchases. People in Finland and Japan can pay for train trips and meals by waving their phone in front of a payment terminal. South Koreans have used mobile phones for cashless transactions for more than a decade. And in the United States, mobile payments doubled from around $500 million in 2012 to $1 billion in 2013.

The value of notes and coins in circulation is now only about seven per cent of the world's total money supply. This saves on printing banknotes and reduces the need to mine the minerals used to make metal coins.

Having more money in digital form might make the world safer. Robberies are less likely if there's not much cash around. For example, in New York City, there were 23 000 reported pickpocketing incidents in 1990, when someone stole cash from another's pocket or bag. Today, such thefts are rare. However, physical robberies of banks or people could be replaced with computer hacking and identity theft.

Digital money won't be good for everyone, though. Homeless people begging for spare change, and charities that rely on coin donations, are likely to suffer when less cash is available. Some people might not trust digital money, and shops might not invest in the new machines required. Cultural traditions will mean that some people will still like to see and feel how much money they have. Plus, half the people in the world don't even have a bank account – and wouldn't be able to live and work in a cashless society.

## Money all around us

These days, cash has been largely replaced by plastic cards. Plastic cards are now being replaced by digital money on mobile phones. Soon you may not even need to reach for your phone or electronic wallet to pay for something. A smart watch, Google glasses or even a ring could store your financial information. Your identity could be verified through a fingerprint, eye scan, voice recognition or DNA print.

Just as a road toll payment can be automatically made using a car's smart tag today, technology could soon be embedded in car windscreens to pay for drive-through meals, petrol or car washes. The same technology could also be used to pay for speeding fines.

The future of money seems a long way from where it began; for example, bartering one goat for six chickens.

# CATERPILLAR SHOES

## Boots that let you relax while you walk

Are you tired of walking everywhere and still too young to drive a car? Then we have the solution: shoes that do the walking for you!

Shoes on caterpillar tracks would let you simply stand still as the tracks transport you. Just as the tracks on a bulldozer let farmers and road workers travel over rough ground, the caterpillar tracks on your shoes would take you anywhere you want. They would also take the energy out of walking: all you need to do is point them in the right direction.

*ARE YOU BRAVE ENOUGH TO WEAR SHOES THAT WALK FOR YOU?*

## Still walking

Caterpillar tracks are a belt of metal plates that replace wheels on bulldozers and tanks. They were named for their movement, because they crawl along like a caterpillar. Invented in England in the late 1700s and early 1800s, caterpillar tracks were being used on British army tanks by the middle of World War I.

The tracks distribute weight over a wider area than traditional wheels. So they are ideal for vehicles driving on soft, muddy ground or rough, rocky terrain – or for shoes that can take you anywhere.

Caterpillar shoes are similar to moving walkways, which quickly move shoppers, travellers and commuters through busy areas. This idea has been taken to the extreme on the Hillside Escalator Link in Hong Kong. A system of moving walkways and escalators transport thousands of people each day, from their hilltop homes to the city nearly one kilometre away.

# These boots were made for walking fast

Although shoes that do the walking for you sound far-fetched, Russian scientists have developed 'Quickwalker' boots that do exactly this. Each time you take a step, the titanium and aluminium boot senses that you have put your weight on one foot. An engine in the boot's heel drives a piston that thrusts down on the ground with enough force to push you two metres into the air. As you take your next step, the other boot pushes down and propels that foot forward. Before you know it, you're taking four-metre strides and moving at 60 kilometres an hour!

Viktor Gordeyev and his team at the State Aviation Technical University, in the former Soviet Union, designed the boots in 1972, but they were a secret until 1990. The Russian Red Army ordered 100 pairs to see whether soldiers could use them to run beside tanks, but army generals decided against them.

## Fuel for a fool

We have the technology to make caterpillar shoes. But the question is: would they be popular? One problem is that you'd need very good balance to stay upright: a walk over rough ground could be quite unstable. Another problem is that although the shoes would take you over rough terrain, they'd be useless when it came to climbing stairs. And then there's the question of the energy source. Quickwalker boots carry a small fuel tank on the side that enables a 20-kilometre journey – but wouldn't using your own energy be better for the environment?

Probably the real reason we don't see people wearing caterpillar shoes is . . . they'd simply look ridiculous!

# BIGGER, BETTER BRAIN

## Improved memory and brain signals

**COULD WE RESTORE A FAILING MEMORY?**

Your laptop is running low on space. The solution is easy: plug in more memory. Could you do the same for yourself to help with your next exam?

## Brain space

But first, how much can your brain actually store? The answer is an amazing amount. Fitting inside your brain are all your memories, including countless songs and their lyrics, people who you recognise in life and on the screen, your favourite books and so much more.

Guinness World Records says that the record for memorising the value of pi (the ratio of a circle's circumference to its diameter) was achieved by a Chinese chemistry student, Chao Lu, in 2005. After four years of study, he recited pi from memory to 67 890 places. That means he correctly repeated 67 890 numbers in a row, in the right order. It took him just over 24 hours to do so.

The human brain contains almost 100 billion neurons. Each of these neurons can form around 1000 connections, which we might think of as data storage. Multiply our 100 billion neurons by around 1000 connections, and the result is 100 trillion pieces of data. That's about 100 terabytes of information (there are 1000 gigabytes in one terabyte), which is far more information than a typical computer hard drive can hold. This is just one estimate of brain power: other estimates range from one terabyte to 2500 terabytes.

## Brain recordings

Researchers are trying to build a device that will record activity from one circuit of nerve cells in the brain, make sense of it, then allow another set of nerve cells to replay it on demand. So far, they have inserted electrodes (wires) into rats' brains and managed to trigger memories – in some cases, creating completely new ones!

The rats had been trained to push a specific lever to get water. The researchers used the implanted electrodes to record the brain signals that occurred while a rat was deciding which lever to press. The researchers then used a drug to shut down the part of the rat's brain that created the signals.

When the implanted electrodes replayed the recorded electrical signal in the rat's brain, it knew which lever to press for a drink. If no signal was replayed, the rat went thirsty.

The implant even helped remind the rat what to do. After a time, its memory of which lever to push faded. A gentle jolt from the implant reduced the memory loss.

A great deal of development is needed before the system could work for people. We already have wireless technology and computer chips that can be inserted in the brain, but there are many challenges to overcome. A person already suffering from memory problems may have brain signals that are too weak to record. And, our brains are far more complex than those of rats.

## Implanting memory

Even restoring some important memories could greatly improve the life of people with a condition called dementia. Dementia affects a person's thinking, behaviour and ability to perform common tasks. Recognising relatives and knowing where the bathroom is would greatly improve the quality of life for such people.

Lawrence Livermore National Laboratory in the United States is developing a device to help restore memory. Similar to the rat brain implant, the device can record and activate nerve cells. The aim is to help people whose nerves are not working properly. Violent blows or jolts to the head can affect the way in which the brain sorts, stores and retrieves information. A disease called Alzheimer's and drinking too much alcohol can do this too.

The idea is that the memory implant will record information and activate brain cells, helping them to overcome faulty connections. This may help people remember information and recall past events.

At the base of the brain is a structure called the hippocampus. The hippocampus is the gateway to the brain's memory – everything that we commit to memory funnels through to this structure. If doctors were to implant a miniature, wireless computer chip into the brain to restore memory, it would need to be placed in the hippocampus. Lawrence Livermore National Laboratory is hoping to begin human trials of this technology soon.

## Bionic eye

It is not just within the brain where advances in computing are leading to breakthroughs. Computing power is helping process information before it even arrives at the brain – in the eye.

Australian scientists are making great progress with the bionic eye, which is a camera attached to a pair of glasses. The camera records the view ahead of the patient, and then sends the images via radio signals to a microchip implanted in the eye. The microchip turns these signals into electrical signals that activate cells in the retina – a light-sensitive layer that lines the inner surface of the eye. The retina passes the electrical signals along the optic nerve to the vision processing centres of the brain. Here the signals are turned into images.

In 2014, Dianne Ashworth became the first Australian to receive a bionic eye. Dr Ashworth had been blind for more than 20 years, but once her bionic eye was in place, she could walk around obstacles without needing her guide dog.

'It's been amazing,' she says. 'The more I've been doing it, the more natural it feels.'

# FLYING WINDMILLS

## Power from windmills in the sky

Imagine a massive power station of the future, up to 28 kilometres across, churning out hundreds of megawatts of electricity to power a small city. You may think you wouldn't want one in your neighbourhood, but you probably wouldn't notice it at all. That's because it wouldn't be *in* your neighbourhood: it would be *over* it, four kilometres above the ground. This is the dream of wind farms in the sky.

CAN YOU IMAGINE A WORLD WITH ENDLESS WIND ENERGY?

## Reach for the sky

United States scientist John Etzler first thought of getting energy from the upper atmosphere using turbines tied to the ground. In 1833, he wrote that we could draw power at 'the heights of the clouds by means of kites'. But it wasn't until 1979 that Australia's Professor Bryan Roberts began developing the 'gyromill' – a cross between a helicopter and a kite.

Professor Roberts built his first gyromill in the early 1980s and tested it in a wind tunnel at the University of Sydney. A few years later he managed to get a large gyromill one metre off the ground, creating strong winds by towing it behind his car along a disused airport runway. Next, Professor Roberts and his team flew the gyromill to a height of 30 metres on windy farmland. By the mid 1990s, they had a prototype gyromill that could lift off the ground, remain stable in the air and generate power.

## Streaming energy from the jetstream

With more than 30 years of research behind him, Professor Roberts is now ready to send a fleet of gyromills into the jetstream. Here, rivers of air race around the globe at a top speed of 500 kilometres per hour. More than 1000 times the power available on the windiest hilltops can be collected in the jetstreams.

There are two main jetstreams: one near the poles, and the other located both north and south of the equator, circling the planet from west to east. This takes them over energy-hungry large cities in China, Japan and the United States in the northern hemisphere, and southern Australia, South Africa and Argentina in the southern hemisphere.

A fleet of gyromills would have spinning rotors that create enough lift to keep them flying. Each gyromill would be tied to the ground by a set of strong cables to stop it flying away. As the rotors spin, they generate power that can be fed down the cables to a ground station and into the electricity grid. A flying wind farm of 10 gyromills would provide as much energy as a medium-sized coal-fired power station.

## Flying windmills? Flying pigs!

There are already balloons tethered at altitudes of up to five kilometres along the United States' southern borders. Known as the Tethered Aerostat Radar System, the balloons carry radar equipment for surveillance activities, such as detecting illegal aeroplanes that may be smuggling drugs. But a balloon large enough to raise rotor blades and generators many kilometres into the sky would be expensive, and kites would need to be huge to carry a wind turbine.

It's not just the cost of construction or practicality of the gyromill idea that's the problem. Although people living close to the wind farm wouldn't hear the rotors spinning and the gyromills would be just specks in the sky, not everyone is keen on Professor Roberts' idea. Aeroplane pilots, for example, may not like his devices coming into their airspace. There's also a limit to the amount of energy that could be generated.

## Power to the planets

Gyromills aren't the only flying windmills on the horizon. Altaeros Energies, a company set up by the Massachusetts Institute of Technology, has developed a floating wind turbine that's a cross between a windmill and a helium-filled blimp. California-based company Makani Power has designed an airborne wind turbine that looks like a 30-metre wing made of carbon fibre. And Joby Energy, another Californian company, is developing a multiwing structure that holds several wind turbines in the sky.

If flying wind turbines can harness wind energy on Earth, they can also work on other planets. Professor Roberts has suggested to NASA that his gyromills would be ideal for drawing energy from the Martian jetstream during a mission to Mars.

# LOSING SLEEP

## Doing away with sleep

IMAGINE STAYING AWAKE 24/7!

We spend about four months of every year doing nothing – just lying in a darkened room, snoring. What a waste of time. Imagine if you could use that time productively. You'd be adding around eight hours to each day: over a quarter of a century of activity to the average lifetime. What would you do with all that extra time?

## Why do we sleep?

The odd thing about sleep is that no one really knows why we do it. But what we do know is that a lack of sleep will make you sick. Too little sleep causes depression, weight gain and mental illness. It also raises the risk of diseases such as stroke, heart attack and diabetes.

In May 2007, Tony Wright, a 42-year-old English horticulturalist, claimed to have remained awake for more than 11 days. He was monitored via a webcam throughout his ordeal. After five days, Tony wrote that he saw 'giggling dancing pixies and elves' instead of the text on his computer screen. He had trouble understanding people. He wrote a blog, although he had to stop on the 10th day when he found it impossible to write anything sensible.

Others who have gone without sleep for long periods report hallucinations (strange visions), paranoia (feeling like someone is out to get you), blurred vision, slurred speech, and reduced memory and concentration. Even one night's poor sleep will probably leave you grumpy, groggy and irritable. Being awake for 17–19 hours straight will make you react as if you have a blood alcohol level of 0.05 per cent. In Australia, that is the legal limit for driving; any higher, and you'll be fined or arrested by the police.

Scientists do have various theories about why we need sleep. One is that the brain needs regular rest to repair itself and keep it working properly. According to this theory, we use up the supplies of substances that the brain needs to operate during the day. These substances, which include proteins and cholesterol (a type of fat in the blood), are replaced while we sleep.

Another theory is that sleep pushes the previous day's events into long-term memory. Support for this theory comes from tests that show people remember information better after sleeping. There's also a theory that sleep is simply a way of saving energy.

## How much sleep do we need?

A newborn human baby may sleep as much as 18 hours a day. Preschoolers need about 13 hours of sleep, primary school students 10 or 11 hours, and teenagers 9 or 10 hours. As people get older, they require less sleep. The average adult needs eight hours, while people aged over 65 need only about six hours.

Animals vary in their need for sleep. Horses only need about three hours of sleep daily, and take naps standing on their feet for just a few minutes at a time. Giraffes sleep for four or five hours a day, while elephants sleep between one and five hours daily. Some bats sleep for 20 hours a day!

At the other extreme, some dolphin and whale mothers and newborns hardly sleep at all – they stay awake for an entire month following birth.

## Sleep less

British prime ministers Margaret Thatcher and Winston Churchill got by on just four hours of sleep a night. United States politician and scientist Benjamin Franklin did the same. How did they manage to function properly?

Sleep scientists have recently woken up to the fact that some people have a gene allowing them to cope with less sleep. Being scientists, they gave the gene the catchy name of *p.Tyr362His*. They studied 100 sets of twins to see the difference between twins with and without the gene. The twins with the gene slept for less time than those without it, and were also better at mental tasks after staying awake for 38 hours straight.

Modafinil is an anti-sleeping drug that is used to improve wakefulness in adults who suffer sleep disorders. Shift workers, for example, may become drowsy because they have to work at night when they would normally be asleep.

In military tests, modafinil helped keep soldiers awake for 88 hours. That's almost four days. The drug helped overcome some of the effects of sleep loss during that time, with hardly any side effects. One soldier reported that modafinil 'keeps you mentally focused when it is hard to stay focused'.

## Sleep more

Despite the efforts to help some people stay awake longer, there's one group of people who need to stay awake less. Most teenagers don't get the roughly nine hours of sleep each night that they need to feel alert and well rested.

All of us have internal body clocks that tell us when to sleep. Aircraft flights across lots of time zones can upset our clocks. So can staying up late, which teenagers often do. Puberty can alter your body clock. Before puberty, most people get sleepy at 8 or 9 o'clock at night. Puberty pushes this time back by a couple of hours, to 10 or 11 o'clock.

Sleep scientists say you can't catch up sleep. That is, a Saturday and Sunday sleep-in won't make up for those late hours during the school week. If you do that, your body clock starts to think that a sleep-in is normal. This makes it even harder to roll out of bed on Monday morning.

You can do lots of things to help yourself sleep. The do's include regular exercise, a healthy diet, a relaxing routine just before bedtime, and dim evening lighting. The don'ts include late-night computer games and action movies, caffeine after 4 o'clock in the afternoon, smoking and drinking alcohol.

So if you're going to invent a way of going without sleep for long periods, you will have to first work out a way of keeping people healthy while they do it. We suggest you try sleeping on it.

# FIND YOUR SECRET
# SPORTING
# TALENT

> **Be a sports champion**

**'We must have perseverance and above all confidence in ourselves. We must believe that we are gifted for something, and that this thing, at whatever cost, must be attained.'**

So said Marie Curie, the Polish-born French physicist who was famous for her work on radioactivity, and twice won the Nobel Prize.

The question for many of us is: what is that 'something' that we are especially gifted at? Could you, for example, become a world-famous basketballer, athlete or swimmer?

There are so many sports to choose from. With a little practice, perhaps you could be an accurate archer, a great golfer or a brilliant badminton player. How would you ever find out if you don't have a go?

If you think it's too late to try a new sport, consider Fauja Singh, from east London. As a child, his legs were thin and weak, and he didn't walk until he was five years old. At the age of 89, he began running marathons. By 104, he had run nine full marathons.

## Practice and pills

From the 1960s to the 1980s, East Germany created the most successful sports system in modern history. This was the time of the 'Cold War', a period of great tension between nations. On one side were the United States and other western countries. On the other side were the Soviet Union and its allies.

East Germany, which sided with the Soviet Union, decided to use success at sport in an attempt to demonstrate to the world the supposed superiority of their communist system of government. As an incentive, East Germany offered money to successful athletes and their families, allowing them to improve their quality of life in those difficult times.

In 1966, East German athletes first attended the summer and winter Olympic Games as a team separate from West Germany. Between then and 1989, they won a remarkable 519 Olympic medals. Per head of population, East Germany gained nearly 13 times as many medals as the United States. Particularly notable was the 1980 Winter Olympics, held in Lake Placid, New York. Here, East Germany topped the medal count – almost doubling that of the host country, the United States.

There were two main contributors to East Germany's success. One was legal; the other was not.

East German sports officials regularly tested primary school children to determine their sporting potential. They sent thousands of promising students, some as young as five, to special sport schools.

The young athletes worked hard and in a very competitive environment, training for up to 40 hours a week. The East Germans spent lots of money on coaches, doctors, training facilities and equipment. The focus was on the high-profile Olympic sports, such as track and field, boxing, swimming, skating and ski jumping. This was the legal part of the sporting program.

The illegal part was widespread doping – giving the children drugs to help them perform better. Girls as young as 12 were regularly given untested steroids, which are chemicals that increase muscle mass and help recovery from injuries. Steroids let athletes train harder and build up more strength. The girls were also given male hormones (chemical messengers that control puberty and development). These drugs had many dangerous side effects, including liver and heart disease, depression, infertility (inability to become pregnant) and miscarriages (failed pregnancies).

This drug program certainly contributed to East Germany's success at the Olympics and at other major sporting events.

## 10 000 hours

It's controversial, but there is a theory that you can excel at almost anything if you are prepared to devote some time to it – 10 000 hours.

In 1993, Anders Ericsson, a Professor at the University of Colorado in the United States, reported on a study of the practice habits of violin students. By the age of 20, the best violinists had averaged more than 10 000 hours of practice each. That's 13 hours every week. The less able performers had done only 4000 hours of practice.

Professor Ericsson concluded that many characteristics that people once thought reflected natural talent are actually the result of intense practice over at least 10 years.

In sport, your body type will have a major influence on your success. Regardless of how much time you devote to practice, if you are only 150 cm tall as an adult, then professional basketball is unlikely to be your career.

## Spotting talent

Body type and natural skills are important in identifying athletic potential. Some (legal) elements of the East German method of screening and training young athletes are still being used today. For example, the best swimmers are usually tall and have long arms. Height is most important for sprint swimmers, while long forearms help swimmers achieve high power and speed.

Elite sportspeople need skills beyond physical strength and natural talent. They also need desire and personal drive to succeed – and to practise, practise, practise. Your body's physiology is also part of the package. This includes how well you can take in and use oxygen, and how well your muscles function.

Diving deeper into the body, can genetic testing reveal your perfect sport?

## Speed gene

Scientists have discovered more than 200 genes that can be linked to physical performance. The best known is *ACTN3*, the so-called speed gene, discovered by an Australian research team in 2003.

We all have the speed gene, and it comes in two forms. One form is called the active gene. It makes a protein found only in fast muscle fibres, which are the parts of your muscles that help to produce explosive bursts of speed and power. The other form of the gene stops that protein being created.

The scientists tested the genetic makeup of more than 300 athletes, many of whom had represented Australia at the Olympic or international level. Ninety-five per cent of those athletes had the active form of the speed gene.

Most sprinters have the active speed gene. But having the active gene won't automatically get you to the next Olympics – billions of people have the active gene and are not athletic at all. We do know one thing, though – if you haven't got the active gene, then you are never going to sprint 100 metres in less than 10 seconds.

The conclusion from this story is – get out and try some different activities. If you enjoy one, keep doing it. Even if you don't turn out to be the next world champion, thousands of scientific studies have shown that working up a sweat is really good for you.

# CLIMATE OF CHANGE

## Coping with climate change

WHERE WILL WE LIVE AND GROW OUR FOOD IN A CHANGING WORLD?

Ice and heat are enemies. As the world warms, the ice on the land melts. Most glaciers are in retreat, with their water gushing into the sea. This makes the sea level rise. Add the expansion of the oceans, which get bigger as their water warms, and we have a significant threat to coastal regions.

More than 150 million people live less than one metre above high tide level, and billions of dollars of homes, businesses and roads are located on the coast. In Australia, about six million people live within two kilometres of the beach. So what can we do when our cities and towns start to slowly slip under water?

## Adapting to a new landscape

Florida architect, Jacque Fresco, specialises in designing cities of the future. He has a vision of floating cities made up of interlocking, cog-shaped buildings.

A company called Freedom Ship floated the idea of an ocean platform more than a kilometre long that would slowly circle the world and could house 60 000 people. The barge would have high-rise apartment buildings, an onboard hospital, schools and a huge shopping mall. But the estimated $11 billion cost may sink this idea before it starts.

What about the millions of people on land who rely on glaciers for their water supply? Farmers in the northern Indian town of Skara grow crops such as barley. The farmers rely on meltwater from the Himalayan glaciers to water their crops. Because the Tibetan Plateau is warming quickly, the glaciers are disappearing, resulting in water shortages in India.

Years ago, an Indian engineer named Chewang Norphel noticed that slow-moving water freezes more readily than swift streams. He used his observation to make artificial glaciers, working with a team to set up canals and divert water from local rivers during winter. The canals slow the water and allow it to freeze. In spring, after seeds have been sown, the artificial glaciers melt and water the fields.

Farming may need to change on an even grander scale as climate becomes more uncertain and the global population grows. Dickson Despommier is an ecologist at Columbia University in New York City. He believes that farms should be vertical, not horizontal. Rather than growing food a long way from the people who buy and eat it, he suggests high-rise city farm factories.

Green Spirit Farms in Michigan, United States, is a three-hectare farm factory pioneer. Opened in 2014, it contains 17 million plants growing hydroponically (without soil) in racks stacked six high. A long-term drought inspired the farm. They recycle most of their water, using 98 per cent less water per plant than traditional farming.

Climate change is an environmental problem that calls for inventive ideas and approaches. It gives us new opportunities to apply new ways of thinking.

# PRINT YOUR PARTS, PERSONALISE YOUR PILLS

## Tailor-made medical support

Today, if you're sick, you need to see a doctor to find out what's wrong with you. You may then take medicine that is known to have a good chance of curing whatever you have. Imagine if instead of having to visit the doctor, we could have our body parts fixed with a bio-printed replacement, our drugs targeted at the specific DNA of body invaders, and our diet personalised to keep us healthy in the first place.

*WOULD YOU WANT A PRINTED BODY PART TO REPLACE A FAULTY ONE WHEN YOU ARE OLDER?*

## Press print

Thanks to advances in 3D printing, the possibility of bio-printing is not far away. Just imagine; there would be no need to join an organ donation waiting list, because you could just print a replacement liver.

Printing bone replacements is already possible. In a world-first in 2012, an 83-year-old woman in the Netherlands had her seriously infected lower jaw replaced with a jaw bone made of titanium metal. A 3D printer made a replacement part in just a few hours, building up the new jaw one layer of titanium powder at a time.

3D body part printing is now advancing rapidly. In 2014, surgeons in the United States used a 3D-printed plastic splint to fix the windpipe of a 16-month-old baby. About the same time, surgeons in the United Kingdom used titanium parts made on a 3D printer to rebuild the entire face of a motorcyclist injured in a road accident. Doctors in the United States also printed a funky pink-and-purple prosthetic hand for a five-year-old British girl born without fully formed fingers on her left hand.

In Australia, science agency CSIRO 3D printed a heel made of titanium for a patient at St Vincent's hospital in Melbourne. The 71-year-old builder, Len Chandler, had cancer in his heel and was facing amputation of his lower leg. Working with biotech company Anatomics, scientists designed and printed the titanium heel, which was then surgically implanted into Len's foot, allowing him to walk again.

Printed artificial bones could one day be stronger than the original human parts that they are replacing. So they could provide improvements, rather than just substitutes.

And how about printing complete organs? The California-based company Organovo prints skin, blood vessels and other tissue for medical research. In future, 3D printers could rapidly replicate objects made of human cells.

## Pop a personalised pill

Your doctor generally prescribes a certain type of medicine for you because it has already cured millions of other people. So the odds are pretty good that it will cure you. But sometimes, a medicine won't cure some people. For example, the common pain-relieving drug codeine has no effect for about one in 10 Caucasian people. Other people are 'super metabolisers' – their bodies process a drug too efficiently. This makes them at risk of overdosing on just one tablet, which is highly dangerous.

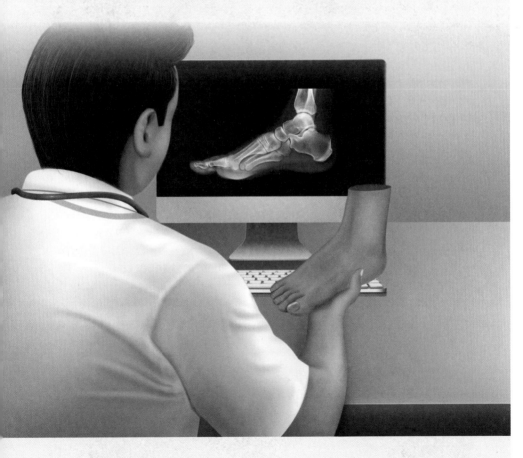

You have about 20 000 different genes in almost every cell of your body. Combinations of these genes influence how you respond to a disease. Now that scientists can decode the DNA in your body, doctors could one day screen all your genes to find out which medicines you best respond to. Once the best types were identified for your type of body, you could be confident that they would not produce any side effects and would cure you faster than anything else. It makes today's prescriptions look like old-fashioned trial and error.

But why stop at analysing the patient's DNA? Scientists could decode the DNA of a brain tumour or other foreign body. They could then design a drug that specifically targets the invading growth or pathogen.

## Fit future

Just as scientists will be able to analyse your genes to work out what you *should* take to feel better, they could also work out what you *should not* take to stay healthy.

You may know some families where everyone lives into their 90s. You may also know families in which many members suffer from a similar disease. This is due to the family's genes, which can influence health and the ability to fight off disease.

However, both nature (our genes) and nurture (what we do) combine to influence our health. For example, some people are not likely to develop diseases such as lung cancer. Not all smokers die of lung cancer, and not all people who die of lung cancer are smokers. But smoking still significantly increases your risk of developing lung cancer.

If scientists could use a simple blood test to identify the diseases you might develop due to your genes, you could reduce your chance of developing that disease by changing your lifestyle and behaviour. For example, about 70 per cent of people suffer from increased blood pressure when they live on a diet that's high in salt. These people would be well advised to develop a taste for salt-free foods.

# SOLAR BLAST

## Power stations in space

**COULD WE GET OUR ELECTRICITY DELIVERED DIRECTLY FROM SPACE?**

Tangles of electric cords from household appliances make a mess and can trip you over. Wouldn't it be convenient if our appliances could be powered through the air? We can connect computers and smart phones to the Wi-Fi at home, and to remote mobile towers and satellites when we are outside. So why can't we access electricity in the same way?

This was a goal of inventor Nikola Tesla.

## A new vision of electricity

Born in Croatia in 1856, Nikola emigrated to the United States in 1884. There he developed new electrical motors and electrical equipment, as well as a wireless guidance system for ships.

In 1901, Nikola built a tower almost 60 metres high above his laboratory in Long Island, New York. On top of the tower was a 20-metre dome. He designed the tower to do two things. One was to send messages by radio across the Atlantic to Europe. The second was to show that it was possible to beam electricity to the homes and factories of New York.

The electricity would come from Earth itself: specifically, from its rotation. Nikola saw Earth acting like a giant battery. His vision was to have towers all over the world, providing energy wirelessly wherever it was needed.

His dream was never realised, because the United States Government dismantled the tower in 1917, during World War I. Well, that and the fact his tower didn't actually work.

## Charging by induction

Wi-Fi and mobile phone transmissions *do* provide wireless transmission of energy. We also receive TV and radio broadcasts this way. However, this energy is too weak to power appliances.

There are some examples of wireless transmission of energy. This is how electric toothbrushes get their power. Inside the toothbrush stand, or cradle, is a wire coil; the toothbrush also contains a wire coil, as well as a battery. When the cradle is plugged into the mains power plug, electricity flows through the coil in the cradle. This causes an electrical current to flow in the coil in the toothbrush, which recharges the battery.

Small powered mats use the same principle to recharge mobile phones. The phone sits on the mat, being recharged wirelessly.

## Space for a new idea

Let's add another element to this invention. Not only do we want to get power wirelessly, we want it from solar cells. No more pollution: just clean, renewable energy for the whole world.

Solar cells are becoming more efficient all the time. The early ones converted only about seven per cent of the Sun's energy into electricity. Today, some solar cells convert more than 40 per cent, and so work much more efficiently.

One drawback of solar cells is that they don't work at night. So let's place them where the Sun always shines – in space! The other advantage of this is to maximise the amount of sunlight hitting the cell; 30 per cent of all incoming sunlight never makes it to ground level. But out in space, there's no atmosphere, clouds or pollution to get in the way.

The downside is the enormous cost of launching solar panels into space – but that hasn't put inventors off. 'SBSP' stands for space-based solar power. When a technology gets an abbreviation, you know that scientists and engineers are giving it lots of thought.

Here's how SBSP would work. You'd have huge reflectors or mirrors directing solar energy onto solar panels. These panels could be placed in a fixed position, 35 000 kilometres above Earth. Or they could be just 400 kilometres up, the same height as the International Space Station, where they would orbit the planet every 90 minutes.

Scientists calculate that solar reflectors 35 000 kilometres out in space spanning up to three kilometres across could generate enough electricity to power a city such as Sydney. But how would the power get down here? That's where the wireless energy comes in. The world's most powerful microwave transmitter would beam power down from a long antenna. The power would travel through the atmosphere and end up at a massive collector on the ground.

The cost? Tens of billions of dollars.

The 400-kilometre, low-orbit option would be lighter and cheaper, although you would need a fleet of units to power a city. Scientists at Lawrence Livermore National Laboratory in the United States have done the calculations. Each unit would have a 70-metre diameter reflector, which would focus sunlight onto a four-metre diameter collector. A two metre wide laser beam would blast the energy down to us. The cost per unit: $500 million.

The Lawrence Livermore scientists say that we might even be able to transmit energy wirelessly from place to place on Earth. They note that wind farms are often located far from the towns and cities that need the power, and

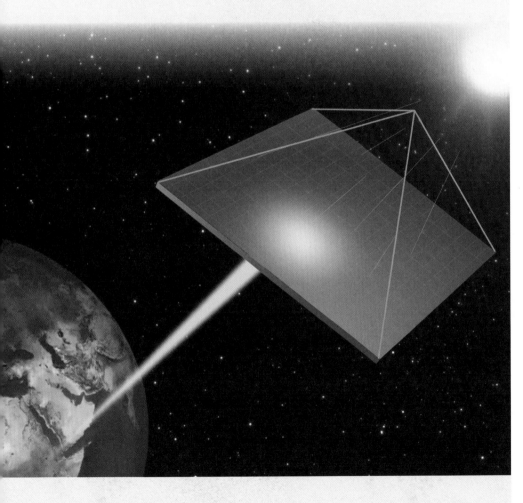

transmission lines to carry the power are expensive. Their report includes a diagram showing a laser beam, which fires energy from a wind farm up to a transmitter on top of a nearby mountain. The transmitter then aims an energy beam down to a city.

## Space wars?

As well as the huge costs, space power faces many other obstacles. What if the high-powered laser beam hits an aircraft or a bird? The laser beam might also accidentally – or even deliberately – be aimed at other satellites, buildings, cars or even people.

If a wireless space energy station was ever built and launched, we can suggest a good name: the Tesla.

# SOUNDS OF SILENCE

## Blocking noise

**CAN WE FIND A LITTLE QUIET IN OUR NOISY LIVES?**

We live in a noisy world. Cars, trucks, planes, sirens, horns, jackhammers, leaf blowers, dogs barking, crows cawing, music blaring – and people around us chatting and shouting, coughing and sneezing. Many organisations are removing individual, private offices and putting their workers into large, open-plan shared areas, which are noisier and have more distractions.

Noise annoys. But it can do more than that – it can kill.

## A noisy health hazard

The World Health Organization (WHO) has found that high levels of noise are causing death and disability in western Europe. Noise is second only to air pollution as an environmental cause of poor health. And so-called 'noise pollution' is likely to have similar harmful effects in all industrialised countries, including Australia.

The WHO reports that excessive noise interferes with people's daily activities at school, at work, at home and during leisure time. Traffic noise harms one-third of the world's people. And one in five Europeans is regularly exposed to sound levels at night that could damage their health.

Too much noise can disturb your sleep and your mind, change your behaviour and reduce how well you can complete tasks. Noise can raise blood pressure and cause stress, even when people are asleep. Over time, fatty materials can build up in the bloodstream and block blood vessels, triggering a heart attack.

The WHO recommends making cars, trains and planes quieter. They urge cities to build noise barriers between major roads and residential areas. Low-noise road surfaces can be made, and quiet tyre designs are available.

## Negate the noise

But let's try to go one better – technology that shuts out noise completely. For example, you could wear heavy-duty earmuffs or earplugs, which prevent some sound from reaching your eardrums. This is called passive noise reduction.

Battery-powered, active noise-cancelling headphones or earplugs go one step further. Like passive devices, they provide a physical barrier, especially blocking high-pitched sounds. At the same time, they actively erase lower-frequency sound waves. Scientists call this clever technology 'destructive interference'.

Here's how it works. A tiny microphone captures nearby noise. Just like ocean waves, sound waves have rising peaks and falling troughs. An electronic system in the headphones analyses the noise waves, marking the patterns of peaks and troughs. It then creates new waves that are opposite to the noise waves. So whenever the noise wave peaks, the electronic waves trough, which cancels out the peak. The headphone speakers play these anti-sound waves, neutralising the noise and allowing you to enjoy some quiet time.

Noise-cancelling headphones can block about 70 per cent of outside noise. They work well in areas with low-frequency sound waves, such as planes, trains and in open offices.

## Zone of silence

Can we have noise cancelling without the headphones?

An Israeli company makes equipment that records and neutralises disturbing noises in offices, kitchens, cars and planes. Microphones track the sounds while speakers play the reverse sounds. The company says that their system can sense and cancel out noise from all directions.

Engineers Joe Paradise and Yasuhiro Ono of the Massachusetts Institute of Technology in the United States have patented a 'zone of silence'. They say that it provides a 'sound bubble' that will let people have private conversations in crowded rooms. The system uses a network of sensors, microphones and speakers to form a 'sound shield' that blasts white noise (a combination of all sound frequencies) and random office noises at bystanders. This drowns out the private conversation of the people in the sound bubble.

The sensors track the people who wish to talk privately, allowing them to move around the room while the masking sounds change direction as needed.

Some people suggest that this sound shield is too complicated. It would be far easier for people to just take their private conversation outside.

## Beam of sound

What if you want music, while everyone else wants quiet? That can be arranged. All you need are directional loudspeakers.

Directional loudspeakers work differently from normal loudspeakers, which blast out sound over a wide area. You can't hear directional speakers – well, not directly. They generate high-frequency sound waves, known as ultrasound. These sounds are too high pitched for us to hear. The high frequency means that ultrasound doesn't spread out like normal sound. It is confined to a beam, like the light from a torch.

Directional speakers actually work by creating an audible sound wave (one you can hear) that rides on an inaudible ultrasound carrier wave (that you can't hear). When the ultrasound beam hits something, such as a wall, furniture or your head, it turns into sound that you can hear. The clever thing is that people standing outside the ultrasound beam hear nothing.

This technology has many applications. It will let you listen to a TV show with no need for headphones and no disturbance to those around you. It could let you focus a spoken message to an individual in a crowd. Museums could play information about an exhibit audible only to people standing nearby. Shops could supply product information to people as they walk by. The driver could be the only person in a car who hears the GPS instructions.

Perhaps directional sound is the answer for those who want a bit of peace and quiet.

# THAT FACE RINGS A BELL

## Face-recognition software

You walk towards your front door. Before you get there, it swings open. As you enter your home, the climate system kicks in. Within minutes, the temperature is just the way you like it. The wall video screen activates, and plays your favourite TV series from the precise point that you got to last night. You sit down on the couch, which immediately adjusts to your body.

**COULD YOU FOOL MODERN FACE-RECOGNITION SYSTEMS WITH A DISGUISE?**

For a while, companies tried fingerprint technology to identify people. But who wants to go around touching germy sensors all day? Instead, face ID software recognises you almost instantly and sends signals to your home system to adjust the room to your liking.

## Facing up to challenges

Humans are very good at recognising people, but it has taken a long time for computers to catch up.

Every face is different. The distance between our eyes varies, and they can be deep or shallow within our eye sockets. Our noses and mouths are different sizes and shapes, and our chins and cheekbones are constructed differently.

The 1960s saw the invention of the first face-recognition programs. Intelligence agencies saw the technology as a way of keeping track of people. The early programs aimed to put a name to an unknown person by matching a photo of their face with an identified photo in a collection.

First, an operator had to carefully mark the position of eyes, nose, mouth and hairline on the photo. Then they measured 20 different distances on the face, such as the width of the eyes or mouth. The measurements went into the computer, which would try to find close matches from the facial data of known people in its photo database. The computer would usually offer up a number of possible matches, and the operator would try to choose from them.

The photo-matching system had many challenges. People could change hairstyles; colour, grow or shave beards; and wear glasses and hats. Features such as the distance between the eyes would be hard to measure in photographs taken from different angles. Head tilt, lighting, photo quality and people's expressions all made the system far from perfect.

Today, we use more accurate three-dimensional (3D) scanning of people's faces. 3D scanning records the shape of the eye socket, nose and chin, which are features that don't change over time. 3D scanning works from different angles and even at night. The approach can match the 3D image with an existing 3D image in a database, or convert the image to 2D to find a match from a standard photo database.

The latest high-powered computer technology can turn a blurry image of a face into a clear one. It can even produce likely matches from a database by focusing only on the eyebrows of a masked person. The best programs can pick someone out from a database of millions of mug shots at least nine times out of ten. And the better the image quality, the higher the success rate.

## Sporting chance

Face-recognition technology scored a publicity boost at the January 2001 Super Bowl in Tampa, Florida in the United States. Police used the approach to scan crowd surveillance images and compare them to a database of digital mug shots. They found 19 people they were seeking to arrest. So it appears face-recognition technology has developed to the stage where criminals can't go to the football anymore.

Police forces worldwide have built up large databases of images. British police, for example, have around 20 million images on file. You probably see face recognition at work every day – for example, Facebook and Picasa software have powerful tools for identifying, matching and tagging faces. Digital cameras have long been able to spot and focus on a face in a scene.

## Body of evidence

Better than a single system is a multiple one. The United States Federal Bureau of Investigation (FBI) has invested $1 billion in face recognition, adding iris (eye) scans, voice identification, advanced fingerprinting techniques and DNA analysis to the mix.

Technology that identifies people from their looks or behaviour is called biometrics. We all know about finger printing, but iris and even vein patterns can also help distinguish us. Other biometric methods include hand scanning and handwriting. Iris scanning involves taking a high-contrast digital image of the eye. About 200 different measurements are involved in an iris scan, with very little chance of mistaking one person's iris for another's. Our vein patterns are also unique. A scanner uses infrared light to take an image of your finger, palm or wrist. The blood in your veins appears black in the scan, outlining your distinctive vein pattern.

Researchers at Carnegie Mellon University in the United States have developed programs that can tell a person's age from a photo by analysing facial lines and textures in nine places around the eyes and upper lip. This approach can even distinguish between identical twins in photos. In a test on pictures of 638 pairs of identical twins, the program identified nine out of ten correctly.

## Smile! You're on camera

Face recognition is rapidly finding new applications. Australian international airports use the technology to quickly clear people through passport control. Video games are just beginning to use it. And some mobile computing devices have even started using it in place of passwords or fingerprints.

Britain has some six million closed-circuit television cameras. That's one camera for every ten people. Londoners and visitors can expect to be filmed or photographed up to 300 times a day. If you visit, make sure you smile for the camera!

# Inventing the future

**We hope that this book on future inventions has prepared you a little for your future lives. Since time travel is unlikely, it's a future you will travel forward towards at the usual speed – 24 hours a day.**

Maybe you've just read these pages in a printed book. Or perhaps you read an electronic version of the text, straight from the screen of a computer or portable device. How do you think people will be reading books in 100 years' time? Perhaps reading won't be necessary at all. If just some of the inventions described in these pages come true, readers in future may download information directly to their brain, bypassing books, screens and even their eyes.

Technology has already transformed our world and our way of life. Many things that you use in your day-to-day activities would be unrecognisable by your great-grandparents. Just imagine what the world of your great-grandchildren would look like to you!

A day in the life of your great-grandchild might start with them sending a thought to their robot servant to say that they're hungry. The robot would print breakfast, which would taste perfectly delicious thanks to new artificial flavours. There'd be no need to clean up after the meal, because all the kitchen's surfaces will be self-cleaning.

After breakfast, your great-grandchild would fly to school, possibly in their driverless flying car. Or perhaps they could breathe through their artificial gills while they swim to school in an undersea community. Their school might even be on the other side of the world: but that won't be a problem, due to teleportation and their ability to take a pill to learn any language. Then, after school, they'd interact with their favourite show on their Holo-TV, and watch it all night because they would have no need for sleep. And they'd do this every day, over and over, for centuries, because they will live forever.

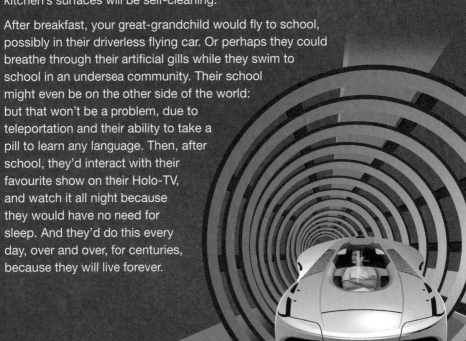

This story of your great-grandchild covers fewer than half of the inventions described in this book. Sure, some of them may be a little far-fetched. But hardly a week goes by without new, exciting breakthroughs being reported in the media, shared online, and appearing in our lives. That's the great thing about human innovation – it never stops happening. Inventors keep inventing. We don't think that there will ever be a day when there's nothing new to invent.

You, as the reader, may even be inspired to think up your own inventions. You might be part of the future solution to many of today's problems. We hope you can contribute to the advances in technology over the coming years – and enjoy them, too.

Our future depends on it.

**– Simon Torok and Paul Holper**

# Imagining your future

Add your own inventions here!